GOING FOR HOPE

STRATEGIES THAT MAKE IT POSSIBLE TO PERSEVERE

GOING FOR HOPE

STRATEGIES THAT MAKE IT POSSIBLE TO PERSEVERE

ANN HOVEY

GOING FOR HOPE © 2024 by Ann Hovey. All rights reserved.

Printed in the United States of America

Published by Igniting Souls
PO Box 43, Powell, OH 43065
IgnitingSouls.com

This book contains material protected under international and federal copyright laws and treaties. Any unauthorized reprint or use of this material is prohibited. No part of this book may be reproduced or transmitted in any form or by any means, electronic or mechanical, including photocopying, recording, or by any information storage and retrieval system, without express written permission from the author.

LCCN: 2024920476
Paperback ISBN: 978-1-63680-398-2
Hardcover ISBN: 978-1-63680-399-9
e-book ISBN: 978-1-63680-400-2

Available in paperback, hardcover, e-book, and audiobook.

Any Internet addresses (websites, blogs, etc.) and telephone numbers printed in this book are offered as a resource. They are not intended in any way to be or imply an endorsement by Igniting Souls, nor does Igniting Souls vouch for the content of these sites and numbers for the life of this book.

Some names and identifying details may have been changed to protect the privacy of individuals.

Dedication

This book is dedicated to my greatest sources of inspiration, my children, Cailyn and Lauryn. You are the reasons I persevered.

I'd also like to dedicate this book to every family we've walked beside. You know first-hand just how deeply this journey challenges and changes you.

Table of Contents

Foreword 9
About This Book 11

Part 1: A Rude Awakening

Introduction 17
How It All Began 19

Part 2: The Acute Phase

Strategy 1: H-E-L-P!!! 27
Strategy 2: Go for Hope! 32
Strategy 3: Focus on What You Can Control 39

Strategy 4: Stay in the Moment! 46
Strategy 5: If You Have an Issue with Someone,
　　　　　　Deal with It! 52
Strategy 6: Embrace the Mindset of Possibility. 63
Strategy 7: Find and Count Your Blessings. 70
Strategy 8: Commit to the Next Right Step 79

Part 3: The Chronic Phase

The New Normal: An Ultramarathon in Disguise 87
Disconnection: Salt in the Wound 106
Long-Term Impacts of Stress 115

Afterword: My Most Important Takeaways 127
　　The Strategies that Make It Possible to Persevere 132
Acknowledgments. 135
About the Author 137

Foreword

I think everyone should read this book. Not even in a "this is my mom, and you should read her book" kind of way, but I genuinely would recommend this to anyone. The strategies my mom presents in the book to cope have been lifesavers on multiple occasions.

There are three parts of this book. Part one introduces you to our story. Part two deals with the acute phase—the strategies we employed during my diagnosis and early journey—and is more about needing to survive the situation in the short term. Part three is the chronic phase—the strategies that focus more on building resilience and lasting coping mechanisms for the rest of your life.

They helped us through medical procedures and through everyday life and continue to do so even years later. I definitely didn't fully appreciate these strategies and all their applications until later in my life—I wasn't yet three when I was diagnosed, and I can't remember a good deal of my early years in the hospital—but now that I'm older, I see the positive impact that these lessons have had on my mom and family. Certainly on me. They've made my mom and I as a unit so much more solid, resilient, and able to approach decisions (medical and otherwise) calmly and generally without conflict. I can't thank her enough for how she has handled everything and continues to be level-headed with me and this journey. The strategies she speaks about in this book really are helpful, and I think I'll find myself employing them in my own day-to-day for the rest of my life.

—Cai Hovey

About This Book

I've been told many times, particularly after speaking engagements, that I should write a book. I struggled with it because I have no interest in simply telling our family's story. I felt that I first had to have a specific way in which I could use our story to help others.

A few years ago, I was asked to speak about building resilient children. At first, I was perplexed at this request because I'd never actually considered what I did to help my kids face adversity with resilience. Still, I agreed to do it and sat down to recount our experiences, along with the lessons I learned. I created and delivered a presentation to a couple of parent groups. I followed that up by creating a presentation on *Facing Adversity to Achieve the Exceptional*. And this led to me hosting four online seminars on *Strategies to Face Situations We All Experience*.

No skill is strengthened without repetitive effort. Although I didn't consciously prioritize building or raising resilient children, I appreciate that the exceptionality of our healthcare journey made building resilience a necessity. We had challenge after challenge to practice how we were going to respond. Over time, the responses that were most hopeful and constructive emerged.

This book is about sharing what I learned through our trials and tribulations. I appreciate that there's no one-size-fits-all way to cope, especially as we all have different experiences and strengths to bring to an adversity. The strategies I share herein are what worked for me and for my family.

If I can help anybody deal with the adversity in their lives, I will have honoured our journey and the lessons I've gained along the way.

Who Is This Book For?

I would like professionals, parents, and caregivers dealing with exceptional journeys and healthcare challenges to read this book. Essentially, it is for anyone who needs a strategy or two to deal with a difficult situation.

In my seminars on facing adversity, I shared personal and professional situations that inspired the strategies I utilized to cope. My focus in this book is to primarily use our personal experiences dealing with my child's life-threatening healthcare journey to showcase the strategies that played pivotal roles in our coping. I share not to elicit strong emotions or pity but because the specific circumstances themselves led to many important observations and personal breakthroughs.

This book is for any one who needs their own breakthrough as they face their unique adversity. The adversity itself doesn't matter. What matters is that we learn about what we need to move successfully through our challenges. Know that you're not alone. And you're doing the best you can.

~ Ann

> *Please Note:* The strategies I'm sharing have made a fundamental difference to our journey. That being said, I believe that, even with the utilization of every strategy, ten children with the same tumour in the same location will have different outcomes.

PART 1
A Rude Awakening

Introduction

This is a story... a true story about resilience made possible by hope. It chronicles moments in a life-changing journey that has challenged me emotionally, mentally, and physically for over twenty years. It details, to the best of my ability, the events, perspectives, and my interpretations along the way.

My particular journey centres on my daughter, Cailyn's, healthcare challenge. I haven't spent any appreciable time contemplating "Why us?" because I don't believe I could find an answer that would make our journey any easier. What I have spent time thinking about, though, is what I need to do to honour this journey. How do I make lemonade out of the lemons that life inevitably brings to all of us? And how do I share my story in a way that could help others at a time when they may need it most?

Every single one of us faces adversity. Often, to move through it, we simply take one step at a time without stopping to consider which specific "strategy" we may have used to cope. My daughter's healthcare journey has pushed me close enough to the edge of my ability to cope that I was forced to look back and examine what worked for subsequent situations along the journey.

In each chapter, I'll share the strategies that helped me—and my daughters—through some of the most difficult moments and realities of our healthcare journey. I had used many of these same strategies over the course of my professional career, but I hadn't recognized them for what they were: simple, powerful approaches to dealing with adversity.

The strategies aren't mutually exclusive. It would be an exception for me to use only one of them in any given situation. I have, however, highlighted the strategies that played the most pivotal role in the scenario described in the chapter. The strategies are presented in chronological order, not by significance. They're all powerful in their own way!

I believe Cailyn's medical team would describe her recovery as exceptional. My greatest hope for this book is that it inspires you to embrace specific strategies for facing the adversity in your life. May you find the strategies that make it possible for you to persevere!

How It All Began

The perspective I share in this book has taken shape over the course of the last twenty years. To set the stage and provide some background, we need to go back to the beginning.

In August 2004, six weeks before her third birthday, my daughter, Cailyn, was diagnosed with a brainstem tumour. The drama of that day in the hospital as we waited for a diagnosis brilliantly foreshadowed the building emotional stress we have experienced hundreds of times since.

My mom had come to the hospital with me, Cailyn, and Cailyn's two-month-old sister, Lauryn. We received our first indication of a difficult diagnosis after our nurse told us the doctor was just heading down to get the results and would be back to talk to us in about fifteen minutes.

An hour and a half later, I was concerned. I told my mom then that it was taking him far too long. Almost a half-hour later, we finally heard his voice in the corridor outside our room. He asked our nurse if there was anyone else in the room. Our concern escalated. Last but certainly not least, we heard him ask the nurse if she would come into the room with him. Our anxiety level was palpable.

Three days after hearing the mind-numbing diagnosis, Cailyn was admitted to the hospital to be prepared for her first brain surgery.

Here are a few things I learned about brainstem tumours in those first days:

1. If this diagnosis had occurred ten years prior, it would have been a death sentence (funny how you can remember the exact verbiage of some things).
2. The brainstem is never a place surgeons want to operate.
3. The doctor thought it was the expansion of the cyst that had led to the quick onset of symptoms, and that reducing the cyst fluid might be the only intervention required at the moment.
4. Cailyn's was a slower-growing tumour, also referred to as a benign tumour. I have grown to detest this term because there was nothing "benign" about my child's journey with this tumour.
5. Cailyn's tumour was surrounded by ten of the twelve cranial nerves leading from her brain to her body, explaining the number of symptoms all popping up around the same time.
6. Chemotherapy is designed to attack faster-growing tumours, so it wasn't a trusted intervention to reduce the size of a slower-growing tumour.
7. Radiation of the brainstem in a young child is only done when it's deemed absolutely necessary because of the likely and damaging long-term side effects.

8. The medical team was hopeful an ommaya reservoir[1] would be sufficient to control the size of the associated cyst, enabling us to manage the symptoms she experienced as a result of the pressure in her brainstem from both the tumour and the cyst.
9. The surgery was to be exploratory in nature, with three objectives: get a biopsy to confirm tumour type, drain the cyst, and insert an ommaya reservoir to enable further drainage of the cyst without requiring surgery under sedation.

Cailyn's first surgery took almost eleven hours. We were gathered in the Pediatric Intensive Care Unit (PICU) waiting room when two women walked toward us. Horrifyingly, we overheard one of them say to the other, "Do you want to talk to them, or should I?" I held my breath until she approached me and told me that Cailyn had made it through surgery safely. Relief... absolute relief... at least for the moment.

While Cailyn recovered in the PICU for several days, we learned that none of the surgical objectives had been fully met. She needed another surgery just eight days after the first one.

This led to my first "tricky" conversation with a medical professional. I was scared for my daughter, as we could see her abilities deteriorate over the week, and I was angry that she had to go through another surgery with all of its associated risks. I needed the surgeon to tell me she was confident her new plan would successfully accomplish all the objectives this time. At the same time, I was afraid of upsetting the surgeon we were relying on to help my beautiful child. I spent a long

---

[1] An ommaya reservoir is a device to facilitate fluid extraction from the cyst

time determining how I should express my concerns so she would be most likely to remain receptive to the message.

I was relieved when the conversation was over, and thankfully, our surgeon understood my concerns, and why it was so important to me that I knew she had a game plan she felt would be successful. I signed off on the surgery. And this time, fortunately, every objective was met:

1. The cyst was drained
2. The biopsy was collected
3. The ommaya reservoir was inserted

After more days in the PICU and on the ward, Cailyn was stable enough to be discharged. Based on what we had learned to that point, we were very hopeful that no further intervention would be required. The ommaya reservoir was in place and could be used to help drain the cyst fluid, and some of these types of tumours grow very slowly. The last item on our checklist was to meet with a seasoned neuro-oncologist. It was during this appointment that our first bubble burst.

The doctor told us in no uncertain terms that Cailyn would not be alive in a year if we didn't find an intervention. After this announcement, I knew what it felt like to be knocked out.

Unfortunately, this wouldn't be our only experience receiving a body blow. One might have thought that our introduction to urgent pediatric healthcare was shocking enough that it would be tough to eclipse it. Let's just say I'm thankful I had no idea what was going to be part of our journey.

Cailyn's next surgery was about two weeks later. The only objective was to reposition a part of the ommaya reservoir, so it was better situated in the cyst and could be more effective at draining it. This was her shortest recovery time, as

Going for Hope

she didn't need to stay in the PICU. We were discharged a week before Cailyn's third birthday. I thought we were on an upward swing.

While this isn't the end of the story—in fact, it's barely even the beginning—it represents a critical moment when my vision for our lives was shattered, and there was no guidebook for getting on with our new reality and salvaging those visions we held most dear. We've all experienced this type of moment. Responding in a hopeful and constructive way doesn't always seem possible, but finding our strategies for moving forward is crucial.

I didn't know what my crisis strategies were at this beginning moment, but through the years, I began to pinpoint the methods that kept me and those around me hopeful, enabling success through perseverance.

PART 2

The Acute Phase

The strategies shared in this section are those that helped me through the first year of our healthcare journey. I refer to this time period as the acute phase because, during this time period, we spent a significant amount of time in a hospital or rehab facility.

Each chapter features the strategy I was most cognizant of using to move through the documented difficulty. In many cases, the title is the actual mantra I repeated to myself.

I have organized the experiences as chronologically as possible. There is some significant overlap, considering more than half of the experiences that inspired strategies occurred in the first couple of months of our journey.

Strategy 1: H-E-L-P!!!

Needing Help Is Not a Weakness

The afternoon we learned about Cailyn's tumour, we spoke with a pediatric neurologist, a neurosurgery resident, and a neurosurgeon. As you can imagine, we had big and mysterious terminology coming at us. Only two things were absolutely clear:

1. Surgery was booked for the next Thursday (eight days away), and Cailyn was to be admitted on the Monday before so testing could be done and conversations could take place.
2. We would be contacted by our neurosurgeon's nurse practitioner (or NP), our primary contact, the next day.

There was very little conversation on the way home. My mom and I were numb and exhausted, trying to process information and a situation for which you could never be prepared. We arrived home to my parents' house after a very long day, just fifteen minutes before our dear friends arrived from Illinois for a planned visit.

In preparation for my meeting with our nurse practitioner, I took advantage of my parents' and friends' wisdom to craft a list of questions. The call was another step along an exponential learning curve. I asked questions; they were answered when a definitive answer was possible. When I asked what the process was going to be when we arrived at the hospital, I learned about the preparatory appointments Cailyn would require before her surgery. When I asked what I could do to best support my daughter, I was told about Child Life Specialists[2] and my ability to speak with a Child Psychologist.

The next morning, I learned that our plans had changed. Our NP called while I was in the shower, and surgery had been moved up to the first thing on Monday. This meant that we were heading to the hospital the next day. So much for a good visit with our friends!

When we got to the hospital on Saturday, we learned that fewer services were available on weekends, including Child Life and Child Psychology. When I realized that we wouldn't be able to avail ourselves of mental and emotional guidance in time for Cailyn's surgery, I sought the help of our nurse. I shared my concern that we were both unprepared. Cailyn had no idea what she would experience both before and after surgery, and I needed to learn everything I could do to best support her through the process. Our nurse understood my concern and left to see what could be done.

---

[2] In both healthcare and community settings, Certified Child Life Specialists help infants, children, youth, and families cope with the stress and uncertainty of acute and chronic illness, injury, trauma, disability, loss, and bereavement. They provide evidence-based, developmentally and psychologically appropriate interventions including therapeutic play, preparation for procedures, and education to reduce fear, anxiety, and pain.

Going for Hope

Later that afternoon, we were visited by an amazing Child Life Specialist who had a comprehensive process, with props, for taking Cailyn through the steps. She had a fantastic way of connecting with Cailyn, and we were both a little less apprehensive about what was about to happen.

I repeated my request to see a child psychologist with each nurse we had that weekend, and during Cailyn's surgery on Monday, I met with someone who would become a critical member of our healthcare team for fifteen years.

Here's the key: When I asked for help, I got it. It didn't always happen with the first "ask," but when something is important enough, you keep asking. I asked *hundreds* of times along this extraordinary journey. I didn't care if the professionals we were working with thought I was a pain. I asked every single one of our doctors, nurses, therapists, and teachers to help me help my daughter achieve her greatest potential... and I didn't just ask them once. In one fashion or another, I asked them about it during every new interaction with them.

I was aware that I ran the risk of annoying someone to the point of alienating them. So, I always asked respectfully and was careful with my tone. I tried to ask for help or answers in a way that I would have liked to have been asked. I also remembered that not getting help the first time I asked didn't mean I wouldn't get it the second time. I had to remind myself more than once that although my daughter was my most important "client," the individual from whom I was requesting help likely had many other clients just like Cai to consider.

About seven years into the journey, Cailyn's diagnosing doctor shared with me that when he first worked with us, he had thought I was crazy. Cailyn was standing beside me during the interaction, so I responded, hoping to dispel the awkwardness, "Well, it takes a little bit of crazy to get through this."

Without taking a breath, he admitted that he had actually felt that I was delusional. He shared that he had been worried that I hadn't been acknowledging the gravity of my daughter's situation. He continued, "You kept pushing us to work with her as if the best results were going to be possible." And then, in his next breath, he gave me a great gift. He said, "Because you pushed us, she achieved things we never thought were possible!" I can't tell you what a difference this made to me. It certainly fuelled my hopefulness and rallied me to "just keep swimming!"

When life challenges you, **ASK FOR HELP!**

It isn't the sign of weakness that we all fear. I've actually come to the conclusion that it's more indicative of an individual's commitment to a better outcome. There are many reasons why it's difficult for people to ask for help. For me, there are primarily two reasons why I have struggled with it in my adult life. First, I feel it's expected of me to have the answer or the ability, and I don't want to fall short of any expectations. And second, I don't always know what help I really need.

This last reason is a very real phenomenon. Along the journey, the offers of help from friends and family were numerous. However, my ability to respond with a specific request for how they could help was very limited. The challenge with an open-ended offer was that I was so overwhelmed by the entire situation that I couldn't begin to process what actionable help could be most useful at that moment. I can remember times when the only answer I could conjure up was a silent scream to "Take away the tumour!"

Regardless of the reasons, this journey made any reservations or concerns I had about asking for help completely meaningless. It was painfully obvious to me that I needed significant help for my daughter to live, so I enlisted the help of every professional we worked with along the way. I viewed each and every one of them as critical members of our team, and I told them so.

Going for Hope

My greatest successes in my professional life occurred when I was facilitating a team towards a significant goal. I have always been certain that the best solutions come when you consider all the pertinent perspectives involved. A facilitator is responsible for how a meeting is conducted, not for what is produced by the participating team members. It isn't the facilitator's responsibility to bring forward the solutions but rather to ensure the process of the meeting uncovers the solutions.

As a facilitator, I never thought of it as asking for help when I was working to inspire the participants' commitment to the process I used. But in hindsight, that is exactly what I was doing. The successes we realized were a direct result of the participants responding to my prompts and sharing their wisdom. Without their involvement, the team wouldn't have achieved its goals.

Practically Speaking, When Asking for Help

When you are facing adversity:

1. Remember, you aren't entirely alone… somebody else has walked down a similar path to the one that you are on.
2. Ask a specialist, a neighbour, a dear friend, or a family member where you might go to get advice or help.
3. Pursue all suggestions that make sense to your particular situation. The more perspectives you gain, the more comprehensive your help will be.
4. Keep a running list of your questions and concerns near to you so it's always available for you to **ASK FOR HELP!**

Strategy 2: Go for Hope!

Things You Never Want to Hear

Our neurosurgeon in London, Ontario, had never surgically been to the part of the brain where Cailyn's tumour resides. As a result, she would not consider "debulking"[3] the tumour, as she didn't want to practice on her. I deeply appreciated and respected her perspective. She felt, however, that Cailyn's best chances required surgery, so she reached out to experienced pediatric neurosurgeons, asking for help. We were in London for a follow-up with her on Cailyn's third birthday when we learned that our timeline for finding a solution was very short. Cai's tumour was developing cysts inside the tumour that were quickly increasing both the size of the tumour and the resulting pressure in her brainstem.

---

[3] Debulking: removing as much of the tumour as is possible, without the intention of a complete eradication; in the brain-stem, there is no redundancy in brain cells, so surgeons attempt to get as much as they can without risking taking any healthy cells

Going for Hope

In the next three days, we had two planned consults. The first was with our surgeon's mentor, who was offering to perform the surgery. Over his career, he had only been to that part of the brain a dozen times, and the success probabilities frightened me. I asked him if he had any knowledge of surgeons who had been to that part of the brain more frequently and could quote better success probabilities as a result. He said yes immediately and then proceeded to tell us about a surgeon in New York. He had sent children to this particular surgeon before and had been very happy with the results.

As this neurosurgeon was offering to perform the debulking, his answer inspired my next question: "What would you do if it was your daughter?" His response was simply, "Take her to New York." He encouraged us to get Cailyn's file sent to this New York surgeon immediately because she needed a solution right away. I called our NP the minute I stepped out of the hospital.

The next day, we had our second consult. This surgeon felt quite differently about Cailyn's prognosis. He told us she had ten to twelve months to live and that surgery would ruin the time she had left. When I asked about the potential solution in New York, he simply stated that he didn't believe it would change his prognosis for Cai.

It felt like we ran full force into a brick wall. Even the kids were quiet on the drive home.

Devastation is a perfect word to describe the mood in our home that night. On top of the fear was a sense of helplessness. Without a solution, I would lose my daughter. I woke up around 2 a.m. the following night to feed Lauryn. Throughout my life, I've experienced my darkest thoughts in the wee hours of the morning, and that night was no exception. I started to spiral downward as my fear for Cailyn grew, and I appreciated in that moment that if I lost her, I might lose myself, too.

Crying, I had a realization that I couldn't falter. I had two girls who needed me. I thought about the book that a friend had given me and that I had read from front to back. Dr. Bernie Siegel's book, *Love, Medicine and Miracles*, documents miraculous medical outcomes. In the wee hours of the morning, I chose to cling to the idea that love and hope can be transformative. These stories Dr. Siegel shared became a brilliant beacon for me, piercing the dark cloud of my thoughts:

GO FOR HOPE!!

It was like someone was yelling at me to not give up and to remind me that, in fact, I could do something. It was such a powerful feeling that I started, right then and there in the middle of the night, crafting a plan. A plan to surround my daughter with hope, believing that her hopefulness would only increase the possibility of a positive outcome. A plan that would get my three-year-old to visualize her tumour decreasing in size. Here's what I did.

I felt an Oreo cookie was a great analogy for her tumour, with the cookie component representing the tumour and the filling representing the associated cyst. I drew what the cookie-cyst combination would look like with each bite taken until no crumbs remained. Hopeful that my plan would help Cailyn understand what it meant to visualize her tumour getting smaller, I felt less helpless. Having completed my drawings, I turned off the light, and both Lauryn and I slept until the morning.

In the morning, with hope, I took two actions: First, I shared my plan, taking the time to explain to Cailyn why we were going to visualize us eating "the cookie." I showed her my drawing of successively smaller Oreos as a parallel to her tumour decreasing in size. Second, I called the hospital to schedule an appointment to discuss Cai starting a chemotherapy protocol. I did these two things in parallel because I understood the gravity of Cai's prognosis and wanted to fight along as many dimensions as possible.

I decided to fully embrace the idea that HOPE is a critical facilitator of achieving good health, and I desperately wanted Cai to do the same.

To remind her to visualize, we shared our plan with every close family member and friend. When these loved ones touched the back of her head and told her that they were taking a bite out of her tumour, Cailyn did the same thing.

While I'd been told chemotherapy wasn't a cure for Cailyn's type of tumour, it was the safest medical intervention available, and we needed to slow down the growth. When explaining to Cailyn why we were starting chemo, I shared that this was another way to take a bite out of her cookie. Learning that many people had defied their odds through hopeful action inspired me to stay hopeful for my beautiful child.

Why did I embrace the concept of hope so fully? My first insight about hope came when I was around five months pregnant with Cailyn. Within the year leading up to this moment, a friend of mine had a jarring pregnancy loss. In a conversation with another friend, I confided that although I was thrilled to be pregnant, I was trying to contain my excitement because I knew there were no guarantees. I shared that I knew how devastated I would be if something similar happened to me.

That's when the insight hit. I realized I would be devastated whether or not I had celebrated, whether or not I was hopeful that everything would work out fine. And this immediately led to my next realization: Staying in the frame of mind where I was hopeful would mean that each and every moment of the journey had a much greater chance of being filled with joy. Dr. Siegel's book *Love, Medicine and Miracles* reinforced that a hopeful frame of mind was critical to achieving unexpectedly positive outcomes.

I have since broadened my belief about hope. I believe it is a critical fuel when facing adversity. When we are hopeful, we take productive and constructive action that we wouldn't even consider taking if we thought there was no point.

I felt strongly enough about this that I told two of Cailyn's doctors that *they* needed to leave room to be hopeful in their conversations with families. One told me they didn't want to contribute to false hope. I immediately countered that false hope was better than no hope. I am sensitive to the pressure that all specialists must feel when they aren't sure of an outcome. Of course, they can't hand out any guarantees! However, maybe they could share the spectrum of possible outcomes they've witnessed if asked by a caregiver what they can expect for their loved one. This way, the "room to be hopeful" could be couched in a way that no one walked away expecting a particular outcome.

It wasn't until years later, in preparation for a presentation to a group of medical residents about partnering with parents for optimal outcomes, that I had a better response to our doctor's concern. I recognized that doctors have actually been trained in the power of false hope because they have learned about the power of the placebo effect. They know that placebos have been proven to be effective with a significant number of patients. Harvard Health reports, "Now science has found that under the right circumstances, a placebo can be just as effective as traditional treatment."[4] It doesn't make sense because it's just a sugar pill, but what gives the act of

---

[4] "The Power of the Placebo Effect," Reviewed by Howard E. LeWine, MD. *Harvard Health Publishing.* https://www.health.harvard.edu/newsletter_article/the-power-of-the-placebo-effect#:~:text=Now%20science%20has%20found%20that,and%20how%20they%20work%20together. Accessed 28 Aug. 2024.

taking a placebo power is that the patient taking it believes that it's going to help—they are hopeful.

During the question period following one of these presentations, a resident reacted adversely to my suggestion that they leave a caregiver room to be hopeful. He stated that they are educated on expected outcomes and consequently would know whether or not someone should be hopeful. I shared that I had been told that my child wouldn't last the year! I used this fact to share my belief that there are no guarantees and no one knows exactly how things will turn out.

"Go for hope" has been my battle cry in my most challenging moments. It cuts through the noise that accompanies fear and uncertainty, and it helps me focus my energy on the constructive actions I might take to open up the potential for a positive outcome. In my darkest moments, when the potential negative outcome was too unbearable to consider, hope turned on the switch to the possible. Going for hope has NEVER let me down, and, in fact, it has fueled my most courageous moments.

Consider the "**Go for hope**" strategy a conscious call to arms when you face adversity. When you do, you keep the door open to optimal outcomes. I feel the opposite is also true for me. If I don't face adversity with the hope that I can create a positive outcome, it's much harder for me to do the things that might ensure the great result I want!

Practically Speaking, When Going for Hope

Critical things to consider:

1. Nothing is written in stone.
2. The "Going for Hope" mindset won't guarantee a specific outcome, but it does facilitate the best quality of life on the way to the outcome. It also means you're much more likely to take constructive and productive action along the way, opening the door for the best outcome possible.
3. There is nothing to lose by embracing this mindset.

Strategy 3: Focus on What You Can Control

Face the Unexpected with Hope

I'd like to share my perspective around Cailyn receiving chemotherapy because it helps you understand my frame of mind during the experience highlighted in this chapter. We started a chemo protocol because we needed to buy some time until a better intervention was available. We chose the protocol that, at that time, had the lowest number of documented long-term negative consequences. Our medical team warned us that it wouldn't shrink the tumour. Still, we began the protocol with the *hope* that this intervention would both decrease the size of her tumour and minimize the potential negative outcomes.

Around midnight on the day Cailyn received her third chemotherapy, she developed a fever and a rash. With the onset of a fever, the protocol is clear—call the hospital. I immediately called the number in our binder for the right contact in London and was told to take Cailyn to our local hospital. After she was admitted, I learned there was one more important step to the process. I needed to call a specific number at our local hospital that would give us direct access to the Pediatric Unit to avoid extended time in the Emergency unit with a weakened immune system. Lots of learning on this journey!

My girls and I were staying at my parents' home at the time, so my dad drove us to the hospital. It was the fastest drive I had ever taken across town with him. We were all scared.

The on-call pediatrician came to the Emergency Department, and things became a bit of a blur. The first priority when an individual receiving chemotherapy gets a fever is to get bloodwork done. Chemo can result in reduced white blood cells, red blood cells, and platelets. If the patient has an infection, combined with decreased white blood cell counts, their body will have difficulty fighting off the infection. Between her lower blood counts, a rash on her torso, and the fever, Cailyn was admitted for the night and started on powerful broad-spectrum intravenous antibiotics. More medical testing was done to determine the possible source of the infection. I can't remember the number of tests, but I do know Cailyn was exhausted emotionally and physically when they were done. I wasn't much better.

The next day, my parents brought Lauryn to the hospital so I could breastfeed her as we waited for information about the type of infection Cailyn had. Her counts continued to decrease, and I felt bombarded with negative feelings of fear, anxiety, and helplessness. This was our first hospitalization for low counts and a fever following a chemotherapy treatment. Thankfully, at this particular time in our journey, I had no idea it would be the first of many. If I had been burdened with that knowledge, I think I might have curled into a ball.

The three of us were in the hospital for three more nights. Thankfully, Lauryn could stay with us because she was breastfeeding. It didn't facilitate great sleeping arrangements, but it meant that we were together as a family unit. It takes time for some of the test results to be finalized, and the protocol for Cai was to stay in the hospital for a minimum of forty-eight hours after she became afebrile (have no fever). Nothing conclusive came out of the testing, and her counts started rising, so we were finally able to leave the hospital and head home... just three days before the next chemo treatment.

Before each treatment, Cailyn underwent bloodwork to see if her counts had rebounded to the level they needed to be to receive chemo. They had, so she had her fourth round of chemo, and we headed home.

Unfortunately, just a few hours later, we headed back to our local hospital with another fever and rash. This time, a concerning consideration was introduced: Did Cailyn have an allergy to one of the chemotherapy drugs? She was admitted, and more tests were ordered.

I'm going to detour a bit here, partially in awe of Cailyn and partially to stand in solidarity with everyone (and every parent) who may have gone through—or is going through—this type of nightmare.

I feel that simply stating Cailyn had medical tests doesn't honour what she went through emotionally and physically to endure these tests. The four types of tests she grew to dislike most—the ones that consequently caused the greatest amount of anxiety every "fevered" hospital visit post-chemo—were bloodwork from her port, bloodwork from an exterior vein, a throat swab, and a nasal swab. She didn't mind the urine samples so much. They were only problematic when she wasn't able to pass urine. After I had explained to her why the testing needed to happen, Cailyn understood that every time she had a fever, one or more of these tests would be required. So, the anxiety ramped up every time we had to head to the hospital with a fever.

Getting bloodwork from a port requires inserting a needle through the skin to a port, often in the chest. The positioning of the port is less than ideal because the insertion of the needle is in full view. And with Cai's port, more than one attempt was required on several occasions to position the needle successfully. Getting blood from an external vein was similarly challenging because, early in our journey, accessing the vein on the first attempt was more the exception than the rule. Not surprisingly, this had a fundamental effect on Cai's expectations for each successive attempt. I held my breath on several occasions.

Considering the difficulties experienced with getting bloodwork done, I'm surprised how upset Cailyn would get with swabs—both throat and nasal. Even with the application of emla cream, a topical anaesthetic, I assumed that the idea of a needle being inserted into her skin was significantly scarier than the insertion of what resembled a q-tip to either her throat or nose. I was very wrong. Cailyn found the nasal swab to be so uncomfortable that she would have easily chosen one of the other "tests" instead. Unfortunately, she couldn't be given a choice.

So, when fevers would occur, not only were our current plans blown up, but my daughter would immediately feel the dread of anticipation for a situation over which she had no control.

Hearing about the potential allergy to one of the drugs scared me deeply. Here we were, on a chemo protocol to buy us some time to find my daughter a better solution, and it was causing allergic reactions that resulted in hospitalizations. I knew there were other protocols, but I understood the list of possible negative consequences with the two other options was longer and more frightening.

It was another moment on our journey when my sense of helplessness overpowered my thoughts. I liken being a parent on this journey to being a project manager of the most important project of my life while having absolutely no control over key variables.

After two days in the hospital, my mom called to tell me that a dear friend of mine was going to take me to a show in Toronto to get me out of the hospital. I told her I wouldn't go. She didn't bat an eye and simply said that she—and another friend—would look after the girls while I was getting a break. She commented that there wasn't anything specific for which Cailyn needed me. She was right, but it was this exact point I was struggling with. There didn't seem to be anything I could do to help my child.

My heart started to race because I felt leaving the hospital was very wrong. How dare I even consider doing something that would normally bring me a sense of fun at a time that was anything but normal and certainly wasn't any fun for Cai? Shopping for groceries the day after Cailyn was diagnosed brought me the same sense of unease. It seemed inconceivable that anything I did would ever feel normal again. It was like there was a distinct wall raised in our lives between pre- and post-diagnosis.

Regardless of my misgivings, I kissed the girls and left the hospital. I fretted the whole drive to Toronto because it was a moment that only thinking, not acting, was possible. And my thoughts were dark. I was afraid we would have to begin a more damaging protocol; I was afraid her abilities prior to her diagnosis might not return; and, most significantly, I was afraid the doctors, who had told me her time was limited, were right.

There were moments during that evening when I wasn't steeped in anxiety. Yes, Cailyn was the only subject over dinner, but I appreciated learning my friend's perspective. I recall sharing my superficial concern that Cai's eyes were turned in and that that was the first impression people would get of her. My friend responded that Cailyn's most prominent characteristic was her personality. It made me feel happy to consider this perspective. In some ways, it was prophetic because it is Cailyn's personality that has significantly helped her face her journey with grace throughout its ups and downs.

The show was also enjoyable. However, it wasn't long before we were in the car, heading back towards the hospital. The closer we got, the greater my unease. I didn't know what the next day would bring in terms of test results or actions. The only thing I did know was that I was heading back into an alternate dimension where I was unable to ignore the situation my child was in, and I couldn't change it.

As I thought about my lack of power to create the outcome I desperately wanted, my anxiety grew. I kept thinking, "What am I going to do? What am I going to do?" Then, suddenly, a sense of calmness came over me. I knew what I had to do. *I had to create a list of the things I COULD do to help my child, and I had to create a second list of all the things in our lives that were blessings.*

By the time my friend dropped me off at the hospital, I had a sense of purpose. I thanked all my helpful angels profusely, kissed my sleeping girls, and, once the room was quiet again, began to write. I wrote for forty-five minutes and generated two lists before I turned out my light.

In the time between leaving the hospital and turning out the light, I had made a 180-degree turn—from desperation to hope.

Focus on What You CAN Control!

The idea that none of us has control over what happens in our lives is an imposing and disempowering truth. The knowledge that we have complete control over *how* we react to what happens isn't exactly comforting. It is, however, empowering.

After I completed my two lists, I felt a sense of calm come over me. It was a moment I will never forget. There have been a handful of moments in my life when I felt confident that everything would work out, and the contrast between this feeling and my earlier deep anxiety was remarkable.

The peaceful feeling I experienced was a direct outcome of focusing my attention on what I *could* control, and it was a portal back to a more hopeful frame of mind. I was still aware that our situation was extremely serious, but in that moment, I made a huge shift from helplessness to "There are things I can do!"

Practically Speaking, When Focusing on What You Can Control

Must do's:

1. Create a physical list of what you can do to help yourself, a loved one, or the situation.
2. Keep it near you and modify it as you continue to learn.
3. Revisit your list whenever you need to be reminded of what you can control.
4. Believe that, with practice, it becomes easier to turn your thoughts away from what you can't control.

Strategy 4: Stay in the Moment!

Don't Let What-ifs Take You Off Course

At this precarious time, Cailyn had frequent scans to track the dimensions of her tumour and cyst. After one of these scans, while still in the hospital for chemotherapy, we were notified that Cailyn had to have her ommaya reservoir accessed to remove built-up fluid in her cyst.

Shortly after being notified, a neurosurgery resident arrived. And I had sirens going off in my head:

- Since he was a resident, there was a good chance this was the first time he would access an ommaya reservoir.
- I didn't have a great working relationship with him, and I could tell he was nervous, reinforcing my first point.
- I added those two thoughts together and was left with one conclusion: He was not the right person for this.

Going for Hope

Our nurse came into the room to apply emla cream to the back of Cailyn's head. Cai's anxiety level rose dramatically because she knew she was about to get another needle.

As we waited for the numbing to occur, the resident said he needed to inform me that there was a slight risk of a brain bleed. I asked him what signs I should be aware of after the procedure. He responded that we would know very quickly because she would die.

My mom was so traumatized she got up and left the room, sending my dad in to be our support. I totally understood why she left. She didn't want to cry in front of Cailyn, who was already in tears, because she was afraid of what was about to happen.

Immediately, my mind careened toward the worst-case outcome. Thinking that the answer would make my decision easier, I asked the resident what he meant when he said there was a slight risk. He said it was about a four percent chance. This response did not provide the peace of mind I was looking for.

I'll share a bit about how my mind works at times. At that moment, I remembered that in my first university statistics course, we were taught that five percent is the delineation between exceptional and non-exceptional. If something happens less than five percent of the time, it is considered exceptional. If it happens more than five percent of the time, it is not an exceptional occurrence.

At the time the resident shared this statistic with me, I was *not* able to celebrate that a brain bleed was an exceptional event. I could only process that four percent was way too close to five, which meant a bleed wouldn't be all that exceptional.

It was an intensely uncomfortable position to be in. On one hand, the risk associated with the procedure was enough to cause me to hesitate. The fact that I didn't think the resident was the right person to perform the procedure added a painful level of fear and uncertainty. On the other hand, I could see the progression of neurological deficits in Cailyn from one day to the next. As the cyst fluid increased, the pressure on the ten cranial nerves surrounding Cailyn's tumour grew, impacting a significant number of systems in her body. Her ability to see, walk, and use her left arm had already declined. Who knew what ability she might lose next?

I felt the crushing weight of the decision and was overwhelmed by the "what-ifs" spiralling around in my head. It all rested on my shoulders. Should I give this resident the authorization to proceed, or should I wait to see if Cai's deficits could stabilize without intervention? The resident was awaiting my decision, but it was so hard to think clearly when fear was running rampant through my head. There were no guarantees that either a brain bleed wouldn't happen or that the intervention would resolve Cai's deficits. The risks and outcomes were both huge unknowns. If there was an ideal solution, it sure wasn't obvious to me.

Feeling powerless, I looked at Cai and realized she likely felt the same way. Her emotional thermostat was deeply correlated with mine. The palpable tension surrounding us wasn't going to ease until I made a decision. This observation knocked me out of my emotional spiral and put me right back *into the moment*. I needed to make a decision because neither of us would experience any peace of mind until I did.

I also felt that I couldn't let Cailyn see (or even think) that her support system was "losing it" because it would only make the situation worse for her. I needed to stay present. Cai's well-being was my inspiration, but staying in the moment was the best thing for me, too! Although it was so very easy to catastrophize, the resulting hamster wheel of emotion compromised my ability to see and think clearly.

With my daughter's emotional well-being now front and centre in my mind, I was better able to assess the situation.

I acknowledged that the potential outcome of the procedure was larger than life, but I could also see the very real outcome of the ballooning cyst. So, it was a choice between potential risk and real need. Looking at it in this way, it became possible to give the resident the authorization to proceed, even with my misgivings. There was no way to know what would happen next, but there was a significant probability of more deficits occurring with the increasing pressure.

Being more grounded in the present, I could interact with Cai more hopefully and constructively. She was afraid about what was coming, and she needed to feel that I wasn't worried, which would have been impossible to achieve if I was thinking about the what-ifs. Her biggest concern was that she was going to have a needle inserted into the back of her head.

I explained to the best of my ability what she would experience. I told her that reducing the pressure in her head would help her see, walk, and use her arm more easily. I assured her that the cream would reduce the discomfort of the needle, so she should just feel a little pressure. I explained why she had to be positioned with her face down and got her to lie across my lap. She stopped crying.

Just before the resident inserted the needle, I told Cailyn I loved her the world full. It was the most important thing for me to say to her *in that moment*.

On the way home in the car, my dad told me I had been a brick. He asked me how I had managed it without breaking into tears. His question gave me pause to consider what it may have looked like to him. He didn't see the frantic spinning of my thoughts; he just witnessed me asking questions, making a decision to proceed, and supporting Cai through the process. Although I couldn't reconcile his perspective with my reality, I was hopeful it meant that Cailyn hadn't been aware of my distress. Dad felt my reaction was exceptional; I felt that it was necessary to minimize Cai's distress. I'm so thankful I was able to stay in the moment because it was the only way I was present enough to say what needed to be said.

Less than a week later, we had to drive back to the Emergency Department in London to have her ommaya reservoir accessed again. This time, the resident on call, someone we had never met, removed six times the amount of fluid that our resident had removed the first time. My mom and I rejoiced on the way home when we stopped for food and saw Cailyn actually use her left hand to eat. We were jubilant because it was the first time in several weeks that one of the obvious declines in her abilities was reversed. At the same time we were celebrating, I felt that we might have been able to avoid the second access if I had made a different decision regarding the first access. Unfortunately, there are no guarantees, and hindsight is 20-20.

Yes, I have learned that staying in the moment is the only way I can bring my best to any moment. It's the only place I have any potential to experience peace, joy, or power. That being said, I have had countless anxious moments when my focus was on one or more fears for the future. So, I sincerely appreciate how difficult it is to stay in this frame of mind. The peace of mind, however, is worth every effort it takes to achieve it.

Practically Speaking, on Staying in the Moment

Presence in the moment, to me, means that I'm fully engaged with what is happening right in front of me. For example, if I'm in a meeting, I'm listening to everything being said instead of planning what I'm going to do after the meeting or what I'm going to have for dinner.

When we are present in the moment, we are more likely to understand the demands of a situation. We can more easily look past our own emotions and consider the needs of others. And most importantly, presence of mind allows us to make the most appropriate contributions, allowing for the best possible circumstances and results.

1. When overwhelmed, take several deep breaths and ask yourself:
    a. Am I clear on the situation?
    b. What is expected of me in the role I have?
    c. What action is required of me in this moment?
    d. Be patient with yourself... it's so very easy to get caught up in what-ifs and potential outcomes.

Strategy 5: If You Have an Issue with Someone, Deal with It!

Don't Let Issues Steal Your Attention

In parallel with the weekly chemotherapy, our neurosurgeon continued to actively seek another neurosurgeon who would be prepared to perform surgery to debulk the tumour. The location of Cai's tumour made the surgery very risky. I was thankful that she was searching because the progression in Cai's tumour was scary.

It was during the search for a neurosurgeon I documented in Strategy 2 that we experienced something quite unique.

Going for Hope

When we arrived at our first consult, I opened the tailgate of my SUV, and *four* dragonflies flew into the cargo area. I could not believe my eyes. As I opened the bag I was going to take into the hospital with us, two of the dragonflies flew out. This seemed so exceptional, and it inspired me to tell my mom that they must be bringing us good luck. A dear friend had told me very early in our journey that dragonflies bring good luck, and I clung to that idea like a drowning person clings to a life preserver. As I walked into the hospital, I wondered if this could be where we were going to get the answer we needed.

Throughout our conversation that day, and after asking some pivotal questions, we learned about the neurosurgeon in New York who had significant experience with tumours in the same brainstem location as Cailyn's. The doctor with whom we were consulting stressed that time was of the essence and that we should ask for Cailyn's file to be sent to this New York surgeon as soon as possible. The minute I walked outside the hospital, I called our neurosurgeon's nurse practitioner to ask for help and trusted that she would follow through.

Ultimately, it was a month after our dragonfly encounter that the information and support provided at this appointment would lead to incredible breakthroughs in Cailyn's journey. I am confident this appointment, beginning with a colorful visit from four dragonflies, resulted in us getting the information we required for her to be here today.

Since this experience, I have embraced each and every moment we have dragonflies flitting about us. We'll take all the good luck we can get!

The day after we got home from the second post-chemotherapy hospitalization shared in Strategy 3, we received a call from our neurosurgeon. She had heard from a different New York-based neurosurgeon than the one to whom we had sent Cailyn's file. She was impressed with his success probabilities for a surgical procedure to debulk Cai's tumour. We booked our flights to New York for a consultation.

After meeting the surgeon, we knew he was the doctor for us. We asked him some tough questions that he capably answered with both humility and confidence. Even still, I had some serious soul-searching to do. I felt he was the right choice for my child, but I didn't know how I would survive the process with all of its dimensions. I had already experienced two episodes of my daughter being in ICU post-surgery, an hour away from home. How was I going to manage when we were nine hours away from home and all our support?

Gut Instinct versus Data

Anyone who knows my educational background might guess that I have a sincere respect for data. I certainly believe that having the right data available makes the best decision or path forward clearer. Unfortunately, having all the pertinent data in front of us, while desirable, is neither guaranteed nor likely.

Our medical journey has reinforced the above truth. I've had some gut-wrenching decisions to make. The fact that I had to make them was sad enough. Adding insult to injury was the fact that definitive data is hard to come by, and no potential outcomes are guaranteed.

Prior to our healthcare journey, when I was trying to decide between two very different professional opportunities, I learned to value information that couldn't be provided by an expert or found in a book.

My decision-making process started with me creating a matrix with the opportunities along the top of the page and life attributes down the side of the page. My attributes included things like: proximity of job opportunity to family and friends, perceived quality of life variables such as the amount of travel and cost of living, and career development considerations.

I lived with this list for a couple of weeks, adding attributes as I thought of them. I then began to rate each of the attributes, recording how well I felt they would be realized in each of the professional opportunities. I eventually added an attribute-specific weighting to the values because some of them were more important to me than others. After totalling the weighted values, I had an overall number for each job opportunity that I was hopeful accurately represented what was best for me.

It was when I looked at the results and acknowledged which opportunity I should accept based on the totals that I became aware of another important consideration: my gut reaction. I turned over the page and theoretically chose the higher-scoring opportunity. As soon as I declared it, I felt an immediate and strong sense of discomfort. This visceral reaction made me think that the higher-scoring opportunity was the wrong choice. The feeling could not be ignored.

My first priority when making a big decision is to seek out any pertinent data I can access from reputable sources. The more important the decision is to me, the more critical it is for me to be informed. What I've gained through significant personal challenges, though, is a healthy respect for my intuition. If I'm having a very strong reaction, positive or negative, to one of the options,

> I need to incorporate this reaction as an important data point.
>
> I have used this approach for other big decisions and have sided with my gut on more than one occasion. Sitting in a restaurant in New York City after our consult with a neurosurgeon, I was struggling to reconcile the terrible prognoses we had received prior to this moment with the hopeful message that this pediatric neurosurgeon could actually help my child. As I sat there, I could recite many reasons why surgery in New York was too difficult to consider. What I hadn't expected in that restaurant was a visceral reaction that strongly opposed my list of negatives. The reaction was, "He is the right guy!" It resounded over and over in my head. This was a data point I couldn't ignore.

It was the biggest decision I had ever faced at that point in my life, and I wasn't the only one who felt its gravity. After I made the decision to take my child to New York, one of our doctors told me that they didn't think they could have made the same decision for their child. The potential cost was just too high (and they didn't mean financially). Boy, did that statement ever catch me off guard! I just stared back at them, not knowing what to say. Their next statement was just as shocking. They said that they didn't believe Cai would live if I didn't take her. At the same time that I was trying to absorb this monumental statement, I worked to internalize it as validation for my choice.

The turnaround between the consult and the surgery was two weeks. My parents travelled with us a few days before the scheduled surgery so that a panel of tests could be done. Then, the night before the surgery, my two brothers and three dear friends arrived. We were not alone after all!

Cailyn's surgery was first on the docket, so it was an early start to our day. My posse convinced me to join them for breakfast, but after a short walk, I felt I needed to return to the waiting room. Cailyn's surgery ended early that afternoon, and I was able to see her just before she was transferred to the ICU. I was shocked when I saw that she didn't have a breathing tube, as she had after two of her exploratory surgeries, and I was ecstatic to hear our surgeon express that he was happy with how the surgery had gone.

During Cailyn's installation in the pediatric ICU, she started to have difficulty maintaining a healthy oxygen saturation rate. According to the Mayo Clinic, normal pulse oximeter readings usually range from 95 to 100 percent. Values under 90 percent are considered low.[5] As we watched her readings fall below 90, the idea of re-intubating her with a breathing tube became a critical consideration.

I agreed with the decision to intubate, and her team suggested I leave the room while they were getting her "cleaned up" (removing all excess tubes, etc.) and intubating her. I returned to the waiting room and spent a few moments with Lauryn, holding her, feeding her, and absorbing her beautiful smile.

Ten minutes before the time I was given to go back to see Cailyn, my older brother told me to go and see how she was. I conveyed what the nurse had told me, and he simply said that he thought I should go. It was really out of character for him, so I did. I peeked into her room from the hallway, and a nurse came over to tell me it would be a little more time. When I

---

[5] "Low Blood Oxygen (Hypoxemia)," Mayo Clinic, March 24, 2023, https://www.mayoclinic.org/symptoms/hypoxemia/basics/definition/sym-20050930.

asked if Cailyn was okay, the nurse replied that she was fine. I returned to the waiting room and relayed the message. My brother asked if I had actually seen her, and I replied that I had.

When I saw her next, she had a breathing tube, and she was extremely upset. For those who haven't experienced this, I can't relay how heart-wrenching it is to watch your three-year-old scream silently. She hated those darn breathing tubes, and it felt like she was screaming at me to do something about it. The medical team had to eventually tie down her right arm because she kept trying to pull the tube out.

I couldn't stay overnight with her in her ICU room and was advised to go out for dinner with my family and friends. I couldn't fathom the idea of leaving her, but her team informed me that, with the drug she was on, she wouldn't remember my absence. They reminded me that I needed to take care of myself so I could take care of her.

At dinner, my mom commented to the younger of my two brothers that he was unusually quiet. He responded that he was just tired from the day. We could all relate! It was an extremely emotional day, but we were thrilled that Cailyn had made it through the life-saving surgery safely.

I arrived at the hospital after breakfast the next day and met with the head of the ICU team. She related that Cailyn had received more of a drug on the previous day than she should have. When I asked what the consequences of this overdose would be, she assured me that there would be no long-term effects. We moved on to discuss Cailyn's status.

When my brothers arrived, they wanted to speak with me privately. I obviously agreed, but I was thrown off by their seriousness. I quickly understood why.

They had been in Cailyn's room on the previous day when she received the overdose... of fentanyl.

Going for Hope

They had watched in horror as Cailyn's oxygen saturation levels dropped from eighty-five percent to eight percent, and a code blue was called. Within moments, a whole team of professionals surrounded Cailyn, doing what they could to revive her.

I told my brothers that I had been informed of the overdose of some drug just that morning but had been given no indication that it had caused something as serious as a code blue. It didn't sit well with me, and I knew I had two options: have a conversation with the ER doctor or say nothing.

Generally speaking, I'm a proponent of directly addressing conflict with someone if two conditions exist: one, if it's likely I'll interact with them many times, and two, if the conflict is significant enough to impact future interactions with them. The exceptions to this approach are if I'm confident that talking with the individual has very little chance of improving the situation and if I'm confident that I can just let the conflict roll off my shoulders, like water off a duck's back.

However, in a healthcare scenario, having a conflict with a healthcare provider brings a whole different level of stress. The last thing I would ever want to do is upset an individual upon whom I rely to provide the best care for my child. This isn't because I expect retaliation; it's just because I fundamentally believe that the quality of care my child receives is optimized when I partner successfully with her care providers. Consequently, the stakes are incredibly high.

I stewed about this situation for a few hours. I felt I needed the doctor to know that I understood the extent to which the drug overdose had impacted my child. I also thought approaching her about it would allow me to assuage my concerns about any potential long-term impacts. However, I was also concerned that making a point of this incident could impact our relationship. Considering our time was just beginning in the critical care unit, I didn't want our working relationship to be awkward or strained.

Shortly after my child was first diagnosed, I begrudgingly accepted my role as her "relentless advocate." Advocacy is the most important role that no parent wants—and they certainly are never prepared for. Although I railed against the need to be an advocate, I recognized that building positive, effective, and respectful relationships with her medical team members required me to embrace the role.

My decision to speak to the ER doctor blossomed from this belief. I was nervous, but I was also hopeful that the conversation would provide assurance that there were no long-term consequences and that this kind of mistake couldn't happen again. I was aware that it would be difficult for me to just forget what happened, so there was a good chance every interaction with the doctor could be negatively impacted by the experience. I also knew that there was a decent chance I would waste invaluable emotional energy fretting about it. This realization gave me the final push. Anything diverting energy away from helping my daughter move forward and heal was wrong. I had to confront the doctor and resolve the issue.

It just so happened that the next time the doctor checked in with Cailyn, I was standing at her bed with my brother, who worked for the organization that makes Fentanyl. I told her that I was glad she had reported the overdose to me prior to hearing about the experience from my brothers because it had scared me to hear about how dangerous an overdose of Fentanyl can be. She had no idea that my brothers had viewed the whole code blue event.

It was important to me to share that I was aware the overdose she spoke of quite casually had resulted in an emergency. She reassured me there would be no further negative consequences.

Going for Hope

I came away from the interaction feeling heard. She seemed to respect me for approaching her on the issue. Stepping up to the challenge of advocating and partnering in my child's healthcare is the most difficult thing I've done. Whenever I felt that a care provider respected what I brought to the partnership, I was inspired to continue stepping up to the challenges.

Feeling like we were on the same page made it possible for me to focus on Cai's needs. Our interaction contributed to a great working relationship going forward. We shared mutual respect, and my input was incorporated into all decisions involving Cai's well-being.

I've come to accept this simple fact: issues don't resolve themselves. They are a subconscious part of our daily lives until we deal with them or dismiss them as not worthy of our attention.

I have had to practice this approach so many times, on both this journey and during my professional career. Having the difficult conversation is never easy, but it does become easier with practice and is always the right choice if the issue isn't insignificant enough to just release it. When my children face this type of decision, I remind them they are worth the effort to address the issue.

Practically Speaking, When Dealing with Issues

How to Prepare for the Conversation:

1. Decide if you need to address the conflict
   a. What impact does the conflict have on the relationship going forward?
   b. Is there a possibility of simply releasing it without any conversation?
2. If you need to address it, first aim to empathize with the other individual
   a. What might they be dealing with?
   b. What could they be feeling?
3. Empathizing can lower your own anxiety or anger and provide additional wisdom on both the real source of the conflict and the best way to resolve it
4. Address it quickly, and remember:
   a. You're worth the effort
   b. It gets easier every time you do it
   c. Continuing to feel the conflict without addressing it is NOT the healthiest solution

Strategy 6: Embrace the Mindset of Possibility

When It Comes to Potential, What Do You Have to Lose?

When we were airlifted back to London, Ontario, from New York, Cailyn was in rough shape. She had left-sided hemiplegia (which is total or partial paralysis of one side of the body), so she wasn't able to crawl or sit up or walk, she couldn't swallow, and she couldn't express herself at the same level as she had prior to the surgery. Because she couldn't swallow effectively, she had a constant flow of saliva down her chin. Countless times every day and night, I suctioned the excess liquid out of her mouth whenever her oxygen saturation stats dropped below ninety-five percent. I didn't need an oximeter to tell when she was starting to choke on her saliva. Seeing your child frothing at the mouth is an experience I wouldn't wish on anyone.

A team of professionals across many disciplines would meet with me on a frequent basis to discuss her progress and decide what was next. Each discussion felt monumental—I felt like we were walking across quicksand desperately trying to reach the goal of my daughter recovering her physical abilities. I remember being asked about my objectives for Cailyn and realizing, as I shared my vision, that I was the only one in the room who felt it was possible.

I also worried about her emotional well-being. The team felt she was clinically depressed but didn't want to medicate her because she needed to fully engage in therapy. It was easy to understand why she was depressed. She went to sleep prior to her New York surgery, able to do the things that a typical three-year-old could do, but woke up with so many deficits. As I held her, she would cry uncontrollably, asking me over and over to hold her because she didn't know how else to ask for comfort… it was heartbreaking.

Before we left New York, Cailyn had a swallow study to assess her ability to swallow. She failed the test. When we were back in London, she went through another swallow study to get a baseline and failed again. As a result, the doctors decided to continue feeding her through a nose tube. She really hated that nose tube and the skin on her face became raw due to her skin's sensitivity to the tape holding the tube in place.

A few weeks after we arrived back in London, we had an appointment with Cai's diagnosing doctor. I asked question after question about her current capabilities and the likelihood that she would recover her abilities. I was relentless. Was Cailyn going to walk? Was she going to be able to use her left arm? Was she going to be able to swallow and, consequently, avoid more surgical intervention? Was she going to be able to express herself? To each question, our doctor responded that he didn't know. In hindsight, I appreciate that he couldn't

Going for Hope

possibly have known the answers to my questions, and it was a more positive response than saying he didn't think these things were possible. But at the time, it was tortuous. I desperately needed someone to say something—anything—that would allow me to retain a little bit of hope.

My frustration at the lack of answers was agonizing enough to spur me to action. After hearing one too many, "I don't knows," I proclaimed quite forcefully, "Well, I know!" His response was also elevated: "Well, I'm glad you know because I don't!" He then asked if I expected a full recovery, and I answered that if it wasn't a full recovery, it would at least be a very strong one. He told me that my response was very pragmatic.

The first six weeks after the big surgery were the most difficult for me. Cailyn was so unhappy that her sadness obscured her brilliant personality and sense of humour. I seriously questioned the wisdom of my decision at the same time that I actively searched for signs that Cai's deficits were lessening.

One of the signs I held on to was the physiatrist's observation that she must be swallowing something because her bib would have been even wetter if she hadn't. Although I couldn't appreciate the difference myself, I was absolutely prepared to accept it. Another sign was an observation I made at the end of her first London swallow study. I got to watch the video of the live fluoroscopy and noticed after she worked very hard for several minutes to swallow, to no avail, that there had been a brief, slight opening of her esophagus in the last minute. I shared my observation with everyone on the care team.

The swallow study was classified as a failure because Cai hadn't successfully been able to swallow anything. But I walked away from the experience, hopeful that the little bit of progress at the end of her efforts was an indication that she just needed to practice swallowing. Until that moment, Cai had received no liquids or fluids orally, so she hadn't used the muscles associated with swallowing since before the New York surgery.

That week, we had another family meeting with all the medical disciplines on our team. One of the items on the agenda was the need to book a surgery to insert a G-tube. The last thing I wanted to consider was another surgery for my child.

Members of her team felt that the G-tube was the best way for Cailyn to get the levels of nutrition required to fuel all of her therapy. They felt that the nose tube wasn't the right long-term answer. I agreed wholeheartedly with this. Cai detested the tube and had tried to remove it herself on more than one occasion. Each time, the re-insertion of a new tube down her throat was a traumatic and painful process for Cai. Her cheek was raw where the tape had been placed and would have to be repositioned on the opposite cheek. I didn't want her to have a nose tube either, but I also wanted to do whatever we could to avoid a potentially unnecessary surgery.

I shared what I had seen during the fluoroscopy and quoted the physiatrist's comments that she must be swallowing something. I asked if there was any way we could "throw this kid a bone." Couldn't we please let her practice swallowing to see if she could further awaken the muscles that hadn't been used for weeks?

I was told that their biggest concern with letting her practice swallowing was that she could end up with fluid in her lungs—obviously not a great outcome. I asked if we could just let her try with a little bit of water every day. We reached an agreement by the end of the meeting and determined the conditions under which Cailyn could practice.

I returned to share the good news with Cailyn and decided to make as much of that moment as I could. I used it to reinforce the point that she had improved to the level where she was going to be able to practice swallowing. Her smile was glorious! And the moment transitioned into a turning point. She couldn't wait to practice, and her mood lifted permanently out of its depression.

Around this time, we were all together as a big family to celebrate Christmas. Cailyn got a day pass so she could leave the hospital to spend the day with her cousins and grandparents at a nearby hotel. Although she couldn't eat, she would scooter herself from one of us to the next to offer her services to feed us the meal she couldn't eat. It was a precious moment and practice for when she was able to eat again!

We practiced, and we practiced, and we practiced (Cai never wanted to stop). The day that we were leaving to head to Bloorview McMillan to begin intense therapy, we had another swallow study.

All of Cailyn's therapists cautioned me not to get my hopes up too high because there was very little chance she would pass, considering how poorly she had done on the previous study. I told all of them that I was hopeful that Cailyn's practice had set her up beautifully for success. A half-hour after the study started, the jury was in: she passed every single step of the test! I witnessed the largest smile I had seen in seven weeks as she received her first tray of food. What a celebration!

What did this reinforce? Well, when you shoot for the stars, you may just land on the moon. I have never been more relentless in my life than when I was advocating for Cailyn, and the vision I was driving towards was her achievement of the best possible outcome. We had nothing to lose by embracing a mindset of possibility, and I never embraced something more exhaustively. The weight of advocacy is real and significant, but it also forced me to bring everything I had learned from my experiences to the table. Anytime I was able to inspire a group of individuals to work towards a common goal, we were successful. I had to try to do the same for my child.

Helping me to stay in this mindset was my memory of a talk-show episode about a boy born without legs. In the show, the father shared that his consistent message to his son was that he could do anything to which he set his mind. His son believed it and went on to blow all the expectations of his medical professionals out of the water.

The greatest message I took from the episode was that we could accomplish great things if we remained hopeful through all the ups and downs and work required. I tried to convey a similar message to my child. I felt strongly that we had nothing to lose by embracing a mindset of possibility because it helped us remain hopeful. Thankfully, Cai agreed with me!

Embrace the mindset of possibility—what do you have to lose?

Practically Speaking, on Embracing the Mindset of Possibility

Embracing the mindset of possibility required me to be hopeful and to focus on what I could control. On our journey, it was painfully obvious that there were exponentially more things out of our control than in it. This can be so disempowering. What fundamentally helped me cope was to focus on specific goals for Cailyn and, for each goal, determine what specifically I could do to support it. The worst thing that could happen by relentlessly striving for the best possible outcomes was that we didn't quite make it to the stars. Thankfully, as our journey demonstrates, in those moments, we at least made it to the moon. Keep the door open in your heart for a victory, large or small.

1. The most critical things to embrace in this strategy are:
   a. Remember that there are very few absolutes in life, and no one has all the answers
   b. Manage expectations because they power our actions
   c. Find a specific goal of meaning to you or your loved one
   d. Determine what specific actions you personally can take to support the achievement of this goal
   e. Be relentless
   f. Celebrate the victories along the way

Strategy 7: Find and Count Your Blessings

They May Be Hiding in Plain Sight, but They're There

We arrived at McMillan Bloorview (now known as Holland Bloorview) later that day. Bloorview is a rehabilitation hospital for pediatric patients. Children could be transferred to Bloorview after their health had stabilized to the point where they didn't require constant acute care. We still had medical professionals attending to Cailyn's health needs, but the focus had shifted to intensive rehabilitative therapy, so most of our days were spent with therapeutic professionals.

In a typical week, Cailyn received physiotherapy, occupational therapy, and speech and language therapy for an hour each and every weekday. By the end of each day, Cailyn would be completely tuckered out, while Lauryn would think it was time to have some fun. We all went to every session—Cailyn wanted me to be with her, and I was allowed to stay because she would work very hard with me in attendance, and Lauryn would be as good as gold. In the four months we lived at Bloorview, there was only one session where Cailyn was non-compliant. As a result, Lauryn and I were asked to leave the room. Cailyn was NOT impressed, but she sure learned from the experience and never behaved in a way that required us to leave again.

I found the first week of our time at Bloorview to be emotionally draining and overwhelming. It started with a series of baseline assessments—one for each therapeutic discipline—to establish a measure of Cai's ability.

There were many moments *in each session* when I was internally screaming at the top of my lungs, "Come on, honey, you can do this... please do it!" I knew from our experience of trying to do therapy at the Children's Hospital in London that if Cailyn was unsuccessful in too many things, she would become irretrievably distressed. I also didn't want anyone involved with the assessment to question her potential, most importantly Cai. After the assessments were complete, we had our first family meeting to discuss our goals for Cailyn while she was there.

I was asked to share what my goals were for my child. I was prepared for the question, and, not surprisingly, as I shared my hopes, it felt like there was a sense I was being unrealistic. I was both sad and concerned for Cailyn; sad because it made me consider that my hopes for Cailyn to regain all her abilities might just be unrealistic, and concerned because I wanted all of her therapists to work with her as if the potential to regain her abilities was a possibility. I can remember feeling quite deflated when the meeting adjourned.

These feelings of overwhelm during our first week were exacerbated by the challenge of figuring out our new "normal" while living in a rehab facility. As a result of her deficits,

Cailyn was about as physically able as her six-month-old sister. Managing little ones provides daily challenges, even when caregivers are at home and have full access to the necessary amenities. Living in an unfamiliar environment comes with additional challenges.

Bloorview is truly an incredible facility, but it's necessarily designed to bring the best level of care to its rehabilitating patients. I didn't expect it to prioritize Lauryn's and my needs. However, that also meant I needed to figure out how to make it work for us, too.

Meals were provided to Cailyn, but Lauryn and I had to fend for ourselves. This was harder on me than Lauryn, as she was just six months old and did not yet eat a variety of different foods. Understandably, I had no idea what to expect this first week and certainly hadn't prepared for a diet of healthy options.

Besides nutrition, good sleep was absolutely critical for Cailyn as she was taxing every aspect of her body and mind with the intensive and extensive therapy she was undergoing. It was imperative that Lauryn and I settle into sleep as quickly as possible to provide a restful environment. Unfortunately, every night-time visit from a nurse shocked Lauryn awake with the bright light streaming in from the hall. Thankfully, these visits didn't seem to phase Cailyn, but they had a significant impact on Lauryn. I was only successful in getting Lauryn to settle into the provided crib on our first two nights.

On our third night, I couldn't rock her to sleep, I couldn't dance her to sleep, and I learned quickly that walking up and down the corridors resulted in a very unhappy and wide-awake girl. In the end, she became my cot-mate. Suffice it to say that getting decent sleep while we were at Bloorview wasn't part of my experience. A thirty-inch-wide cot with a sweet little being nestled beside me just didn't allow it.

Going for Hope

Another challenge was determining the best solutions for Lauryn to be mobile. Being in a hospital environment, I felt I couldn't allow Lauryn to crawl freely on the floor of any room we were in. Unfortunately, she was at the age when that was exactly what she wanted to be doing. Lauryn would only stay on her blanket on the therapy room floor for a period of time. Eventually, she would set her sights on getting closer to her sister—crawling on the institutional flooring and distracting Cailyn. When this happened, Lauryn was moved to our stroller and got to watch the rest of the therapy session from there. I'm sure it wasn't an ideal situation for her.

The sleeping arrangements, along with having to contain Lauryn more than she wanted, forced me to consider other possibilities. A couple of my friends had suggested that Lauryn stay with family and friends so she could be spared institutional living. Having more complete information about what our living arrangements entailed, I had to face this concern squarely and assess the intelligence of my decision.

Compounding the stress of adjusting to our new world was the reality that we didn't have the same daily, unsolicited, and hands-on support from our loved ones. We had experienced an amazing level of support during our time in London and New York, and living at Bloorview was a sharp contrast. Many families experience this phenomenon when dealing with a similar health journey. Help—in the form of extra hands and an ear to talk to—is plentiful when your loved one is in an acute phase of an illness. And the help comes naturally, usually without having to ask, which is a huge blessing because, as I've shared earlier, it's very hard to even figure out what is truly needed.

There are fewer hands and ears when you have moved on to a less acute phase because there is a perception that moving out of an acute care hospital means that things are returning to normal. On a side note, I have yet to meet a family going through this type of experience whose life returns to normal. Unfortunately, there's a new normal we need to accept, and it requires moving through a few stages of grief to get to the point of acceptance. It's a very long road of ups and downs.

So, at the end of our first week, I was struggling with living at Bloorview with my two girls. I was concerned about Cailyn's health and her capacity to recover her abilities; I was challenged with balancing Lauryn's needs with Cailyn's. I realized what a difference it made to be in my own space with access to all the amenities we have at home, and, last but not least, I was a wee bit fatigued. Still, I felt I was coping… and then we had bath night.

The room where I could bathe the girls was a decent distance down the corridor from our room. With their current level of abilities, there was no way I could safely manage both girls without our little bath chairs, which I did not have. I decided Cailyn would go first, so I left Lauryn buckled into the stroller. After getting Cai in the tub, I realized I left something we needed in the room. I obviously couldn't leave the girls in the bathroom by themselves while I ran down the hall, so I got Cailyn out, dried her off enough to get her clothed and back in the double stroller, and wearily trekked down the hall.

An hour later, all three of us were exhausted—Cailyn due to the physical and mental wear and tear of all of her therapies, Lauryn from crying because I wouldn't let her crawl all over the floor, and me from all of the shenanigans. When we got back to our room, Cailyn fell asleep almost immediately.

While I walked the floor in our room with Lauryn, I began to feel very sorry for myself. I was emotionally and physically exhausted, and I felt alone. I was in a position where I was always "it" and always on. Being "it" takes on a whole new dimension of challenge when it involves life-altering decisions and situations. I didn't know how I was going to survive the months ahead. I was afraid for Cailyn and worried about Lauryn. My emotions started to spiral downward. Then, as I was desperately trying to stay in control of myself, I experienced a stab of insight.

My turnaround began with the realization that, at this moment in time, I was with my two beautiful children. And I was at the beginning of a significant block of time when the three of us would be together as a team, without the distractions that come with "normal life," such as Cai going to preschool or me going to work.

This thought reminded me of a phrase I'd heard hundreds of times growing up: "Start at the other end of the stick and count your blessings." Every time my mom told me this, she was asking me to consider the blessings I had in my life as opposed to focusing on the problem I was experiencing at the time.

It was a surreal moment. In less than a minute, I went from frantic to calm. I honestly don't know what initiated the a-ha moment. It could have been divine intervention, or it could have been growing up in a home where problems were often referred to as opportunities. In that instant, it didn't really matter what initiated it—what mattered was that my emotional outlook made a 180-degree turn.

All of a sudden, I was acutely aware of the biggest blessings of living at Bloorview. I had an invaluable amount of time with my girls, and at the same time, Cailyn was receiving the level of therapy that could give her the best chance at recuperating her abilities. With this realization, the door to feeling sorry for myself was shut and locked from the other side.

I'm not going to say we didn't experience challenges during the remainder of our stay in Bloorview. What I will say is that, while we were there, I never went to the dark place of feeling sorry for myself again. This moment of clarity highlighted the fact that our time at Bloorview, regardless of how challenging, was the facilitator of two significant blessings: Cailyn received the intensive level of therapy she needed, and I got to spend time with my two kids. Once I had this realization, I couldn't forget it.

Also imprinted on my mind was the dramatic difference in my sense of well-being that I experienced when I focused my thoughts on my blessings. If I couldn't get back to sleep after waking to feed Lauryn, and my concerns got the better of me, I would begin a breathing routine. I would breathe in for a count of four, hold my breath for a count of four, and then, as I slowly expelled the air, I would say "thank you" for one of my blessings.

Admittedly, there were times I had difficulty completing the first breath. I couldn't land on a blessing. These moments happened frequently enough that I decided to choose a default for them. When I struggled, I would start by saying thank you for my strength. Once I got started, each successive breathing cycle became easier. Sometimes, it only took ten cycles to relax to the point where I could fall asleep, and sometimes, I lost count of the number of cycles needed to achieve enough peace at that moment to fall asleep. Remarkably, it always took only a handful of full-breath cycles for me to experience an improved mindset.

Counting my blessings is not always easy. As a matter of fact, there are times that it feels damn near impossible. Regardless of the emotional effort required, I'm never sorry after forcing myself to go through the process. Going through it either slows my heart rate and thoughts or fills me with the sense that I can do what it takes to get through the moment. Sometimes, that's all that is needed. And I've learned that the more I am struggling with a situation, the more critical it is for me to stop the downward emotional spiral by thinking about a blessing.

Going for Hope

Proviso: I don't know if I would have had any capacity to count my blessings if I actually lost Cailyn to this horrible illness. Thankfully, my ability to get to a more positive state of mind through this strategy hasn't been put to this horrifying of a test. I know that this strategy has worked for me when I was feeling very desperate, but losing a loved one brings on a whole different level of pain and struggle. If this strategy could bring even the slightest bit of relief to someone who has lost a loved one, I would count that as another one of my blessings. When I consider the families we've met who have lost children, I marvel at their ability to persevere in honour of their children.

I am so very thankful for Bloorview. Over our four months living there, the intensive level of treatment provided by our amazing therapists was instrumental in helping Cailyn build enough strength and stamina to regain her ability to walk and use her left arm, among many other skills and abilities. Most importantly, she regained her ability to express herself at a similar level to which she could understand, removing the deficit that most negatively impacted her emotional well-being. And I had many opportunities to create and practice a process for getting myself to a more positive frame of mind—all through counting my blessings.

Practically Speaking, When Counting Your Blessings

I seriously understand how counting your blessings can be the absolute last thing you would think of doing when facing great adversity. Why the rounds of breathing work for me:

1. The breathwork involved quiets my mind and slows the racing of my heart.
2. Forcing myself to think of one blessing after another reminds me that there are good things in my life, too.
3. My frame of mind is fundamentally and noticeably improved after ten cycles of breathing and saying thank you. This reality is actually quite significant considering the states I am usually in when I begin the process!
4. During the day, it helps me get on to doing something constructive, and at night, it helps me fall asleep.
5. So, when you're experiencing some form of distress
    a. Breathe in for a count of four
    b. Hold your breath for a count of four
    c. As you release your breath, for as many counts as it takes, say "thank you" for one of your strengths, blessings, or opportunities

Strategy 8: Commit to the Next Right Step

Perseverance is Accomplished One Moment at a Time

While living at Bloorview, when Cailyn's health was stable, we were able to leave the hospital to go home and experience "normal" over a weekend. The primary idea behind this was that the child would unknowingly be getting therapy while they were doing the things they would normally do at home. We all loved being at home, and the reasons are both obvious and too many to list. That being said, it was difficult to embrace that our normal was now different in ways I never imagined or wanted.

This truth created cognitive dissonance. I was very happy to be home, but being home forced me to acknowledge how much our normal had changed. It was a difficult reality for me to accept.

One afternoon during a homestay, after putting Lauryn down for her nap, Cailyn asked me to take her to the bathroom. Getting to the bathroom on our main level requires going down four steps. I transported her down the stairs and waited. Typical of my approach with Cailyn, I decided we were going to fully embrace the idea that she could continue her therapy while at home.

I reminded her that she had done a great job the past week relearning how to crawl, and I told her that she was going to build on that work by crawling back up to the main level. She did *not* like the idea and insisted she was not going to crawl up the stairs. She asked me to pick her up.

I told her I wouldn't. I shared how proud I was of the hard work she had been doing and how happy I was for her that her efforts were helping her become stronger. As I walked to the top of the stairs, I asked her to think about the fact that she hadn't even been able to crawl until the last week. And I pointed out to her that it was her determination and perseverance that had changed that. I told her that all her improvements had been as a result of her trying.

She asked me again to come down and pick her up. I told her again that I was not going to pick her up because I believed in her. She was *not* impressed. The biggest disconnect between us was that I was confident she would be able to do it, but unfortunately, she wasn't. It didn't help that she wasn't able to see all of her accomplishments objectively. I was stubborn and outwaited her. And she made her first attempt. As I shared earlier, Cailyn's left side was extremely weak, so when she placed her left hand on the first step, her elbow buckled, and she stumbled. This is when the crying started.

I felt I was emotionally at the edge of a cliff. I so wished I hadn't made such a big deal of it. I just wanted to pick her up and hold her close, assuring her that she was okay.

Going for Hope

Unfortunately, making such a big deal of both her ability and the benefits of all of her hard work placed me firmly between a rock and a hard place. I had no idea how I was going to get us both out of the situation gracefully.

At that moment, I had to choose the best next step, which meant that I needed to take a deep breath and make sense of the competing concerns.

On one hand, I didn't want to heap on additional trauma to the substantial pile Cai had already amassed. Regrettably, at this point, the situation was already stressful. On the other hand, both my professional experiences and our family values inspired me to consider pushing forward.

As an organizational coach, I have had many conversations with leaders about the importance of saying what we mean and meaning what we say. It's very difficult to sustainably lead people if you don't do what you say you're going to do. And I caution them that they marginalize the power of their words when they don't follow through or when their actions contradict their words.

On the home front, two of our family values are Integrity (say what you mean and mean what you say) and Perseverance. Both of these values had something significant to offer to the moment. On the integrity front, I had just said things to Cai that I didn't want to be marginalized by my action or lack of action.

As I mentally recounted what I had said to her, I knew there were a few things that my next action absolutely had to reinforce. She couldn't question whether or not I believed in her ability to accomplish what she worked hard to do. I also didn't want her to question whether she had actually made real progress. The expression "in for a penny, in for a pound" resounded in my head as I committed to what I was going to do.

I walked down the stairs and explained I wasn't going to pick her up, but I would add a little bit of stability by holding on to the waistband of her leggings. She really disliked that idea, and the crying escalated to a loud enough volume that I expected Lauryn to wake up from her nap.

Speaking very quietly, I told Cailyn that I knew she could do anything she put her mind to. That's what came out of my mouth, but on the inside, I was feeling a bit like a monster. My child had been to hell and back over the previous six months, and I really just wanted to pick her up, cuddle her, and tell her I loved her.

Regardless of my serious misgivings, I continued talking to her quietly and encouragingly as I walked back up the stairs. I sat on the floor and prayed that this wasn't going to be the stupidest thing I had ever done. I kept calmly reinforcing that she could do it while internally screaming, "PLEASE, PLEASE, PLEASE!"

Minutes later, Cailyn was sitting in front of me with the biggest smile on her face. To say I was beside myself with gratitude would be an accurate description. I gave her a huge hug and asked her what she was feeling, and she said simply, "I'm proud of myself." I don't have the words to express just how relieved I was. The moment is forever etched in my mind. Seeing the joy in her face was the best possible ending to a significant moment. And it gave me the opportunity to tell her that she had just proved to herself that working hard towards a goal gave her the best chance of achieving it.

As an aside, I have to add that this whole experience was made possible by hope. With everything that Cailyn had been through, I would never have suggested that she try to crawl up the stairs if I had felt it was an impossible ask. When it all went awry, I wanted so badly just to pick her up and hold her. And that is exactly what I would have done if I wasn't truly hopeful that she could be successful. Without hope, I would have whisked her up as soon as she became upset, regardless of whether or not it conflicted with the wisdom gained through my professional experiences. My hopefulness is what fueled my action and made Cailyn's experience possible.

That particular weekend, we didn't work on any other major milestones. Any therapy happened only as a by-product of having as much fun as possible. But back at Bloorview, Cailyn had a new light in her eyes. She had fully turned the corner, earning her therapist's observation that she had never worked with such a determined and motivated three-year-old.

This experience reinforced the importance of perseverance. Cailyn had to persevere to get herself up the stairs, and I had to persevere to take the best step in that moment... the step that made it possible for Cai to solidify her understanding of the positive difference that perseverance could have in her life. What a wonderful springboard to more success!

As she dealt with persistent and extensive physical challenges, Cailyn's understanding of this difference was tested over and over again. While we were at Bloorview, it was easier for Cailyn to stay in the mode of working and strengthening. Persevering became harder after we were discharged from Bloorview. After reintegrating into the outside world, she was surrounded by able-bodied peers and family members. It was obvious to her that she had to work much harder to do everyday things than anyone else she knew.

In theory, all the opportunities to practice perseverance would strengthen the "muscles" required to constantly rise to the challenges requiring it. And I think that would be the case if other factors didn't come into play. Two of these factors are the need for ceaseless stamina and resilience to rise over and over again, as well as the ability to ignore the thoughts that life just isn't fair.

Perseverance is required to accomplish new goals and abilities, and it's also required to get through difficult situations.

An unfortunate irony is that we most need perseverance in the moments when the idea of persevering can seem beyond us.

At these times, I try very hard to breathe deeply and commit to taking one step—THE one step that is most important to take in that moment to move through it. When I take that step, I recognize it as me doing my best to persevere.

It's much easier said than done, especially when I'm worn out or sad or afraid. But when I commit to only one thing—the right thing to do *in that moment*—and if I try, try, try, I will likely prevail.

Practically Speaking, on Persevering

Must dos in a stressful moment:

1. Take a deep breath. Allow the breath to quiet your mind. This makes it possible to be in the moment and see it for what it is, not what it might turn into.
2. Consider either what the moment requires you to do or inspires you to do.
3. Act with hopeful intention so you can persevere.

PART 3

The Chronic Phase

In the last part, each chapter shares key strategies for moving through significant challenges during the first months of our healthcare journey. These first eight strategies met our needs in those specific moments.

In this part, the chapters focus on the fallout of our healthcare journey. The intention of these chapters is to shine some light on the unanticipated difficulties faced by families like mine over the long term.

I would never have thought our new normal could present so many difficulties. Learning about these new difficulties is one thing. Accepting them is another. And embracing them is a whole different beast!

We return to our homes, families, friends, and some of our old routines, but it can feel alien, like an alternate dimension.

The New Normal: An Ultramarathon in Disguise

Even After Everything, You Still Grieve What You've Lost

This chapter easily took me the longest to write. I struggled with it because I felt the additional weight of honouring every other caregiver who has wrestled with the challenge of embracing a "new normal"—a new reality that none of us would have ever willingly put on our vision boards. The intention of this chapter is to shine some light on the types of things we face that magnify the challenge of reintegration.

As I noted earlier, everyone's healthcare journey is unique. Not everyone responds well to the same medicines, has the same modalities of care and team members, or follows the same recovery plans. But everyone experiences the stresses of navigating the complicated world of healthcare, coping with the unknown, and reconciling the resulting changes to their lives.

I believe our new normal began after we left Bloorview, almost nine months after Cailyn's diagnosis. I struggled with being discharged because Cailyn was still working very hard in her sessions and hadn't plateaued in her abilities. I felt Bloorview was the best place for her to regain her strength and ability. That said, I truly welcomed the idea of returning to our home. It was a very big moment; not only had Lauryn spent seven of her first eleven months of life in a hospital or rehab facility with her sister and me, but we were returning to a different house. Three of my dear friends managed our move to a new home while my girls and I were in the hospital.

As we got in our car and drove west towards home, away from the safety net of professional care, I believed we were going back to our normal lives. It didn't take long to learn that there was no seamless path back to our "pre-diagnosis" life.

Our time at home started with sincere gratitude for the simple things, like visiting with our loved ones, sleeping in our own beds, and having relatively easy access to our favourite foods. But the fabric of joy at being home was gradually pierced with small but unmistakable holes. These holes didn't obscure how wonderful it was to be home, but they were hard to ignore. And, as the number of holes increased, the fabric of our lives seemed both less recognizable and less stable.

Every experience that challenged us in a way we couldn't have imagined prior to the diagnosis created a hole. I asked four caregivers, who have become dear friends, what aspects of returning to our new normal were hardest for them.

The weight of advocacy we all bore coloured our thoughts on the transition. As I've hinted at, being an advocate is the toughest and most important role I've ever had to play. As an advocate, you are the project manager of likely the most important project you will ever have. And the caregiver in this role has no control over many of the critical deliverables.

Our joint responses can be grouped into the following adversities. As I drove home from Holland Bloorview, I had no idea how challenged I was going to be by any one of them:

Adversity #1: Ongoing Neurological Deficits

I'll generalize here, but for many caregivers, the following list is all we know about our child's neurological deficits when we arrive home:

- There is no guarantee of further improvement.
- New deficits can develop over time (and have physical, intellectual, and emotional impacts).
- The window for regaining strength and ability is limited.
- Any improvement will require real and sustained therapy.
- We are now 100 percent responsible for facilitating that therapy. Without unlimited funds, daily, hands-on therapy from a specialist is impossible.

After being home for a few months, I learned that the list also included:

- Having the responsibility for driving and overseeing all of Cailyn's therapy truly overwhelmed me. I didn't feel I had the luxury of relaxing our efforts if there would be any chance for Cailyn to recover her full strength and ability. The action of "fitting therapy into" our daily life was a serious stressor due to the ticking clock. It was a balancing act, and I went to bed many nights feeling like we had failed that day to do what was needed to achieve the ultimate goal.
- I wasn't going to be the recipient of the amazing focus and effort Cailyn had given her Bloorview therapists. My three-year-old "client" didn't appear as determined and

motivated as she had been at Bloorview, and there were definitely moments when the adjective compliant could not be applied. I finally clued in: she wasn't as dialled in because she didn't want me in the role of therapist. She simply wanted me to be her mom. Needless to say, bedtime came before exercise completion for the majority of our days.
- Another important contributor to Cailyn's reduced focus was that determination can fizzle over time if obstacles keep presenting themselves. And life at home brought with it a revolving door of new obstacles. In the hospitals and rehab facility, Cailyn's and my focus was necessarily inward, on anything and everything going on with her health and therapies. Any interaction with other families was incidental and stayed on the plane of a passing social interaction. It wasn't until we returned home that our myopia lifted, and we engaged more purposefully with our social network. This is when I started noticing all the differences in abilities between Cailyn and her peers. I held my breath because I knew it was just a matter of time before she started seeing it, too. Even though it was inevitable, it was heartbreaking when she did. It became one more outcome, directly resulting from her healthcare journey, for her to accept and withstand. Her sadness at this realization necessarily required me to develop coping strategies for both of us. Her need for continued therapy to close or at least reduce the gap added further insult to injury.

In our first months home, before we started going to our local Children's Treatment Centre, KidsAbility, Cailyn received formal therapy from the local hospital twice a week. She worked so diligently in these sessions to regain strength in her hands, feet, arms, legs, and torso. However, the novelty of receiving hands-on therapy while living at home wore off quickly, as she didn't have obvious improvements to celebrate each session. Cailyn would leave a session simply fatigued, not victorious, and neither of us wanted to even consider the list of exercises to complete before our next session.

How do you explain a marathon to a three-year-old? You can't appeal to their ability to understand what's at risk, especially when it's impossible to know yourself. I couldn't begin to estimate the number of times and different ways I used to inspire her to work. My relentless focus, fuelled by my concern for her quality of life, was exhausting for both of us.

Now, it wasn't without its blessings. Every time Cailyn realized an improvement after working very hard to achieve it, she was reminded about the power of perseverance.

It would be terribly negligent of me not to highlight how amazingly Cailyn rose to impromptu requests to do something therapeutic. I couldn't even estimate how frequently I asked her to turn her left foot outward, to place her heel down first, or to use her left hand. What made it most exceptional was that she never gave me any attitude. And it's even more exceptional considering how long therapy was on her "must-do" list. She must have had negative thoughts, but I certainly didn't hear them. I doubt anyone could have managed my incessant encouragement better.

This doesn't mean I didn't get any attitude about other things, like homework, because I certainly did. But it seemed that when it came down to doing something intended to make her stronger, she would buckle down.

Adversity #2: Continuation of Medical Interventions

Our family schedule was riddled with frequent medical and therapeutic appointments that made it impossible to ignore the difference between our new normal and our pre-diagnosis lives. The medical disciplines involved with Cailyn's ongoing care included oncology, neurology, neurosurgery, ophthalmology, orthopaedic surgery, endocrinology, cardiology, psychology, neuro-psychology, and others, if you can imagine.

In the first years of our new normal, we were in London (an hour and a quarter-minute drive without traffic or bad weather) for a follow-up appointment anywhere from once to several times per month. Sometimes, we were able to coordinate more than one follow-up per trip to keep the trips down, but I also recall being in London three separate times in one week.

A critical component of each follow-up is a physical assessment. On days when the specialist was working with a resident, the assessment would be done twice: first by the resident after they gathered Cailyn's health history and then by the specialist.

I couldn't possibly estimate how many times Cailyn had to hear me recite her story. I'm sure she got tired of hearing it, and I certainly felt the pressure to relay anything of potential importance to elicit the most accurate interpretations and guidance. Distilling Cailyn's journey down to what I felt was the bare essentials never felt right. With the sheer volume of things she had experienced, I always felt that the superficiality of sharing a few bullet points fell far short of honouring her journey.

I often wondered if Cailyn felt the same way, but I learned many years later that her coping mechanism of choice was to tune us out. She inadvertently revealed her approach after an appointment with her orthopaedic surgeon. I asked her on the way home what she thought about the doctor's suggestion that surgery would be necessary if we couldn't achieve the desired strengthening of her left foot through physio. She was flummoxed. She hadn't heard the word surgery once, and the doctor had mentioned it a minimum of three times.

Going for Hope

After the history gathering and physical assessments, there was time to share observations and concerns and ask questions. My preparation for an appointment always involved the creation of a list of observations and questions, as well as a summary of any significant insights coming out of appointments with other specialists.

This part of the appointment was particularly difficult for me because there were so few answers available. That's one of the things you learn on this kind of journey. You can meet another individual with the same tumour in the same location, and the outcomes can be very different, making black-and-white answers impossible. As I found out early on, the lack of answers can be extremely difficult, especially when the questions have to do with your child's quality of life and long-term potential.

For all of Cailyn's specialist appointments, her current status and her potential to regain her strengths and abilities were the most frequent topics of discussion. A less-voiced but ever-present concern was whether there were any indications that Cailyn's overall health and strength were at risk of worsening, either due to tumour growth or her current deficits.

The emotional energy consumed during each appointment was significant. I can't imagine how difficult it was for Cailyn to have the kind of attention no child could possibly want, but it definitely took a significant chunk out of me. Whether the day involved one appointment or multiple, I needed a few days to recover my energy.

As a result, I was always hopeful that there was nothing of consequence on our schedules in the few days following an appointment because all I really wanted to do was hibernate. Manufacturing excitement for a school concert or recital seemed impossible. And it wasn't just an energy thing. There were also times that it was just emotionally difficult to reconcile the contrast between the worlds of the hospital and whatever was on the docket of normal life. The challenge of embracing our new normal was draining.

Adversity #3: Risk of Relapse and Progression of Disease

The mental, emotional, and physical actions required to support Cailyn through the above adversities felt all-consuming. Unfortunately, the level of emotional energy needed to stay vigilant about any new developments eclipsed both of them.

In general, I'm a very positive person, hence the reason I had some specialists thinking I was crazy or delusional (or both) for constantly asking our team to sign up for my vision of Cailyn's exceptional recovery. Regardless, I can totally relate to the expression, "once bitten, twice shy." I will never forget hearing the news that Cailyn had a tumour. And our journey has taught me that receiving that kind of news once leads to many similarly difficult conversations with specialists.

Besides the challenge of remaining positive and hopeful with recovery and appointments, caregivers are responsible for paying close attention to any potential changes in our child's health, abilities, or behaviour. It's a juggling act to keep hopefulness in the same headspace as vigilance, and it's a challenge that's impossible to conceptualize if you haven't been through it. I felt like our life was a crash course in tightrope walking. While shaking with physical and mental effort, balancing on hope seems impossible.

I'm confident I'm not the only parent who has found it difficult to walk the line between being present in the moment, enjoying it for what it was, and remaining vigilant to any signs of a concerning development. It is an unenviable situation to be in—wanting to stay in our happy place but having to be on the lookout for signs that could shatter our sense of happiness in the wink of an eye.

Adversity #4: Unexpected Triggers and Challenges

Some of the emotional challenges caregivers face are much less obvious. These represent some of the more unexpected trials I encountered.

- The weight of advocating within the hospital and across all medical specialist appointments is significant but somewhat predictable. What I never anticipated was how critical advocacy would be at school, at therapy, and with extra-curricular activities. To achieve the best potential outcomes and a desirable quality of life, our kids need to receive the necessary level of support in these realms, too. Advocacy is a constant need.
- My professional experience facilitating teams taught me that optimal outcomes are more likely when every team member's perspective is considered and everyone is striving for the same outcome. Along our type of journey, each medical specialist, therapist, teacher, educational assistant, and coach is an important team member. As the only people present at each interaction with every team member, it's incumbent upon us caregivers to ensure any important information from one team member gets shared with all other pertinent team members. Never have I felt more driven to do what I could to facilitate the best outcomes possible. Unfortunately, wanting to facilitate the best outcomes meant I had to accept the accompanying pressure. I certainly couldn't anticipate how much my energy would be zapped through all our interactions.
- Grief pops up at both expected and unexpected moments. The obvious moments are when we learn about another consequence of either the tumour or the interventions. These moments make you grieve the loss of a "perfectly

healthy" child. The not-so-obvious moments come from situations that prompt the "what might have been" questions or make it possible to observe the differences between your child and their peers. I have used a roller-coaster ride as a metaphor for Cailyn's and my journey together. I remember the first time I realized it was a perfect reference. One doctor had made subtle allusions that the only way I wouldn't be worried about something related to Cailyn's health and well-being would be if she weren't here. At the time, it felt like a punch in the stomach, but when I had time to process it, I realized it was just a statement of fact. A life with a brain tumour involves long-term effects. There's no way around it. So, you have the highs of wonderful experiences with your child, but they are accompanied by the lows of walking beside them as they suffer with ongoing consequences and realities. There is an unavoidable cost for a longer ride. I grieve the resulting costs even while celebrating Cailyn's presence in our lives. When I feel overwhelmed by my sadness for something that she is dealing with, I remind myself of the families we have met who would do anything to walk beside their child again, regardless of the challenge.

- I'll never forget the first time while sharing the results of Cailyn's MRI, I heard the doctor say that the stable MRI was a reason to celebrate. I had sincere difficulty accepting this as a reason to celebrate. From my perspective, the only outcome worthy of celebrating was noticeable shrinkage in the tumour, an indication that the tumour was becoming less viable. It also made me wonder if our medical team felt the best we could hope for was "stable" if it was so worthy of celebrating. I knew that as long as the tumour was viable, it could grow again and require more serious intervention. I needed this thing to GO! I was obviously happy that the tumour hadn't noticeably grown, but I wasn't jumping up and down that the tumour was stable. In my mind, no obvious growth in the tumour didn't slam the door hard enough on the potential for future progression.

An unexpected outcome of the conversation was my observation that medical professionals can't possibly understand how difficult it is, as a caregiver, to manage all the emotional aspects of this type of journey. Certainly, most haven't had to live through their own version of it. Over time, my understanding grew. First, I eventually grasped the fact that medical professionals have been privy to so many situations that truly are so much worse than a stable MRI result. No wonder they feel a stable result is worthy of celebrating! And second, after three more tumour progressions, I eventually appreciated just how wonderful a stable MRI result actually was.

- For significant health issues, an increased expenditure of emotional energy is sustained over time. The drain of energy would certainly be higher on a day that we received bad news or had a difficult procedure done, but overall, the outflow of emotional energy remains higher than normal. Over time, it seems to take less and less trauma to experience exhaustion.

Earlier in our journey, I hadn't yet learned how fundamentally my emotional energy level impacted my physical and mental energy. This lower level resulted in noticeably reduced physical and mental stamina, which affected every part of daily life. If I had known and respected this relationship, I am hopeful I would have been much more conscientious about two things: first, managing my emotions around a specific event, and second, actively releasing the negative energy through exercise.

As far as feeling is concerned, I acted instead of felt in the heat of the moment. I didn't consciously choose action over feeling, but in our most difficult moments, my focus on Cailyn's needs didn't leave any room for feeling. In some instances, the rush of emotions would happen hours after a traumatic situation or a difficult conversation with a medical professional. There have been other times when the rush of emotions came years later, but only once I allowed myself to reflect on what happened during a difficult moment.

Regarding exercise, after a long day dealing with difficult news or situations, the last thing I wanted to do was engage in exercise. I already felt "done," so it wasn't even on my radar to do one of the few things that could help release the built-up stress.

Unfortunately, not acknowledging my feelings didn't mean my body wouldn't have to deal with the consequences of having them.

- A very real challenge of returning to normal for many caregivers is coping with the reality that even our closest relationships don't understand how deeply affected we have been and continue to be. Being understood is a critical psychological need, and I learned how fundamentally it supported my overall sense of well-being. It wasn't until the first time I was socializing with other families on similarly challenging journeys that I learned just how precious a gift it was. Appreciating that it's very difficult to be empathetic when you haven't walked the same path doesn't always soften the sting of not feeling understood.

Adversity #5: Walking the Tightrope Between "Normal" and Respectful

A strong piece of advice received from our Child Psychologist early on in our journey was that it was emotionally healthy for Cai to experience as normal a life as possible. Had her new normal not included things like tumour progressions, years of weekly chemotherapy, and recovery from several surgeries, this task might not have seemed so herculean for both of us. I can't imagine what thoughts went through Cai's mind, but I could understand why she would wonder out loud if achieving normal really mattered.

Regardless of my acute awareness of the uniqueness of Cailyn's experiences, I tried to honour the advice to push for normal. Some examples of my efforts were that I had many conversations with her about honouring her intelligence and taking homework seriously. I would push her to go to extracurricular activities if she was well enough to attend. I expected that she would treat others the way she wanted to be treated herself.

But reconciling hospital days with school days had to feel impossible for Cai. One day, she's sitting in a classroom with her peers, and the next day, she's in a hospital, praying that her port will work the first time it's accessed. The trauma of the access was only the tip of the iceberg because, on hundreds of occasions, it was the precursor to receiving chemotherapy.

It was nine months into a chemotherapy protocol that Cailyn learned that we were not going to be stopping her weekly chemo regimen after the two-year mark. Being several months into the weekly protocol, she was devastated by this news and told me that her life "officially sucked." A few weeks later, pushing for normal, I asked Cailyn to focus on the math sheets she had brought home in preparation for a test. I asked her to choose a couple of questions per section and to write out the answers formally on a clean sheet of paper. I told her I'd be happy to help if she had any questions.

Over thirty minutes later, she was still sitting there, having done nothing except complain about having to do homework. She could have been well on her way to finishing if she had applied her energy toward doing her math. I couldn't understand why she was wasting her time because we had agreed that she could be free to do whatever she wanted after she finished. When I next checked on her, I noticed she'd scribbled answers in the margins of the prep sheets. Not only was it difficult to decipher, but she was also unsuccessful in showing she knew the material.

As I became more frustrated, she became more belligerent. More loudly, I asked her to honour her strengths and take the test preparation seriously. She looked at me indignantly, and I knew that she had no intention of following through. I had a lightning bolt thought: This wasn't about any specific homework. It was about how she couldn't possibly care about how well she did on a math test when her feelings about her life were so negative.

I changed my approach. I sat down and quietly told her I appreciated how difficult it must be to care about something like math when her life sucked. She nodded.

I told her how sorry I was that she had such unfair cards in her hand. I told her I would take them away in a heartbeat if I could. I asked her to believe me when I said that everyone has crappy cards, even if their specific cards aren't obvious to us. I asked her to consider the other cards in her hand because she has some brilliant cards, too: her intelligence, her sense of humour, her determination, and the love and support she has from her family and friends. I asked her to accept that she could decide which card she focused on, and I told her

I hoped she'd look at her brilliant cards because they would bring her some happiness instead of sadness.

Her math sheets were finished with no further argument or hesitation. The interaction ended well, but not without both of us experiencing distress. I felt I needed to support her emotional well-being by expressing normal expectations, but this was in sharp contrast to what Cai needed at that moment: to feel understood. Balancing the often opposing priorities has challenged me innumerable times across this journey.

Strategies

Since arriving home from Bloorview, I have used many different strategies numerous times to help me reconcile a particular development, incident, or concern with our new normal. Unfortunately, the fallout of this type of journey is both significant and unexpected. You never know what's around the corner, at the next appointment, or after the next scan. Yes, because of the once-bitten, twice-shy phenomenon, we no longer live with the assumption that our good health is a given. But, even so, difficult news slams into us like an out-of-control vehicle.

Coping with the news isn't a one-time thing, either. We may experience the greatest shock when we first hear it, but we are immersed right back into the feelings of concern, fear, or sadness each time the consequences of the development touch our day-to-day lives.

When I have spoken to groups of medical professionals on the importance of partnering with parents, I share that I was still learning, years after Cailyn's diagnosis, what it meant to have a child with this diagnosis and to be thrust into this new normal. It felt like each insult had a cumulative effect, and coping strategies were instrumental for me to maintain any semblance of hopefulness.

When the need for action collided with one of the above difficulties of our new normal, I was only capable of productive and constructive action once I had managed my emotions with some strategy. It's very difficult to prioritize non-health-journey-related tasks when drowning in a pool of fear, concern, or sadness. Actually, it's hard to even care about them at all.

Over time, we become clearer on our go-to strategies. Across the months and months of struggling with our new normal, I have used many, but there are four I would classify as my most utilized and effective approaches for combatting ongoing feelings of fear, concern, sadness, and grief.

The first and likely most powerful is the deep-breathing technique I described as part of strategy seven. I don't believe, after all these years, that I have used any other strategy more frequently. My approach to deep breathing is a fantastic way to focus my attention on the blessings in my life. When I first started using this strategy, I will admit that there were many times I struggled to find one thing for which I was grateful. It may have taken dozens of breaths to reach a sense of calm, but it always worked.

A second strategy I first read about online is one I personally refer to as "five by five." Not remembering where I first heard about it, I went searching online and found a reference to "The 5 x 5 Rule." Whether or not this is my original source, the concept resonated beautifully with me when I first heard it.

The wisdom I gleaned from what I read was that I shouldn't worry for more than five minutes today about something that won't be an issue in five years. This strategy has been very effective at putting problems, issues, and concerns into perspective almost immediately. For the issues that pop up and elicit a singular emotion, like frustration or concern, this strategy has operated like a reset button for me.

A third strategy I've used when dealing with multiple emotions was one that got me through a difficult situation in my first job after graduating with my Masters degree in Statistics. I refer to it as my "Black Box It" strategy.

I had wanted a job for the summer after I graduated to raise money for my trip to Europe. My dad arranged for me to go to one of his plants and apply my education to the improvement of the manufacturing process. I had no experience with this process, I was fresh out of school, and I had no street credibility. The fact that process experts hadn't achieved the desired quality improvements after several months of analysis was daunting. I did *not* want my dad to end up with egg on his face. That first week was tough. I couldn't imagine what I could possibly add to the situation. I was confident that everyone in the plant questioned my presence, just like I did.

A week into my experience, I had an a-ha moment: thinking of all the ways I was challenged was taking up valuable energy—energy that I needed to put towards helping improve the quality. I decided that I needed to put every single insecurity into a black box on a high shelf and not look at them again until after the project was completed. I knew my insecurities weren't serving me, and I visualized putting them in the box and locking it. Once I did that, something clicked. I don't know what it was, but it freed up my attention to focus on what I *could* control. It was only then that I could determine what my "next right step" was.

In the end, we achieved a remarkable improvement in the quality. Along the way, I gained the understanding that my ability to make a critical contribution had everything to do with me "black-boxing" all my negative feelings and insecurities. Until I did, I couldn't clearly see what I needed to be doing to make that difference.

This particular strategy opened the door to effectively utilize another strategy: "focusing on what I could control." There are challenges we face where one strategy just simply isn't sufficient.

Throughout Cailyn's journey, I was frequently swamped with difficult feelings and insecurities about the inability to do what was necessary to help my child achieve sustainable health and well-being. Determining what I might do to make *the* difference for Cai's health and well-being was hidden behind the noise of fear, sadness, worry, grief, and frustration. In this headspace, it's impossible to see the best path forward.

The difference between my first real work challenge and my role as Cailyn's advocate is that my feelings and insecurities experienced through our healthcare journey wouldn't stay in the black box. Difficult emotions would rise with every new health development. So, Cailyn's healthcare journey has certainly given me significantly more experience with lassoing my emotions than my professional challenges ever did. Thankfully, every time I practised this strategy, I freed my mind to figure out what I could do to help. It worked beautifully in moments when my emotions were spiralling.

I refer to my last strategy as my "hand of cards" strategy. Simply evoking the phrase "hand of cards" speaks volumes to both my kids and me. It's so very easy to focus on the negative stuff. Unfortunately, focusing on the positive in light of a negative situation requires conscious effort. When I utter this phrase, it's simply a way for me to reset my thinking. Being aware of our difficulties and dwelling on them are two very different things. Thinking positively doesn't necessarily erase the difficulty, but acknowledging our brilliant cards can be very empowering. You can't capitalize on strengths you aren't acknowledging.

Practically Speaking, on Adjusting to an Undesired New Normal

Upon learning of a challenge, you need to:

1. Take several deep breaths. This can fundamentally calm your mind and facilitate clearer thinking.
2. Understand what you know about the challenge and decide if you need more information to begin dealing with it.
3. Once we have all the information we need, use the Five by Five Rule:
    a. The answer to "Is there a significant potential this will be an issue in five years?" should determine the level of effort we are prepared to exert to address the issue.
        i. If you answer "No," maybe addressing the issue can be as straightforward as evoking the mantra, "Don't sweat the small stuff."
        ii. If you answer "Yes," more effort is required on your part to facilitate the best outcome.
4. If significant effort is required to contribute to the best outcome, black box any insecurities hampering your hopefulness and focus on what you can control.

Disconnection: Salt in the Wound

I use the phrase "emotional isolation" to describe how I have felt after unexpected interactions with cherished friends and family members. I experienced a sense of disconnection every time I walked away from a conversation, believing that I hadn't been able to communicate either what I was feeling or what I was coping with at the time.

Being "heard" on this type of journey is so critical. Those involved experience the fallout of the journey on a daily basis, and it's hard to ignore the continuing barrage of resulting emotions and realities. So, it's not difficult to comprehend why we would want our loved ones to understand our situation. I wouldn't have experienced this sense of disconnection from a casual acquaintance because there was no basis upon which I'd expect them to "get me."

Going for Hope

I've rewritten this chapter many times, searching for better words and phrases. Why? Well, the moments of emotional isolation I've experienced across our journey have tested me significantly. The sense of disconnection was distressing enough that I needed to figure out how to cope.

I know other families on similar journeys have also experienced challenges with their support system. My hope in explaining these struggles isn't to place blame but rather to shed light on this unexpected by-product of our journey and share the strategies that worked for me.

Wanting to be understood was a powerful drive for me. Some of that drive was fuelled by the need to be understood, and some of it was inspired by my need to release the difficult emotions. The emotions accompanying these trials don't resolve without a conscious effort to clear them. I embrace the adage, "A trouble shared is a trouble halved." It must be based in truth because sharing is one of the best ways I've found to work through my feelings about our adversities.

Anyone who has dealt with life-changing adversity is likely to deal with some form of emotional isolation from their existing support base. Even in situations when you're not the only one going through a particular adversity, you're still the only one who understands how the experience is pushing your buttons and impacting your overall well-being. Considering the concerns on my radar related to everything my child was going through, I would never have imagined that my sadness and confusion over this sense of disconnection could be significant enough to take up *any* space on my emotional radar, but it did.

If emotional isolation had been an expected repercussion, it wouldn't have been so tough. The weight of the unpredictable physical consequences and mental gymnastics that our journey triggered made sense. Experiencing a sense of emotional isolation from some of my closest relationships completely blindsided me.

The sense of emotional isolation stemmed from three sources.

The first was my own inability to find the words to describe exactly what it was I was feeling. The longer the time between interactions with someone dear to me, the greater the pile of thoughts, feelings, and concerns waiting to be shared. It was as impossible to summarize our situation effectively with one thought as it was to vent "everything." My challenge was exacerbated by my diminishing well of energy. Determining my feelings and crafting a clear summary of emotional events took an amount of emotional bandwidth that I didn't always have.

The second contributor to the sense of disconnection was the fact that there were physically fewer opportunities to share. Juggling get-togethers was tough with the larger list of to-do items on our calendar, and admittedly, my desire to socialize was lower than normal. It's hard to have your feet in two extremely different worlds: one in which you get together with friends and family with the express purpose of enjoying each other's company and one in which the idea of enjoyment seems like an impossible stretch. During some of the more challenging moments, it simply felt wrong to have my attention split between my children's needs and an "enjoyable" diversion.

I did attend special social events, and I tried my best to stay in the moment. Inevitably, someone would ask how we were doing. The dearer the relationship, the greater the drive to vent anything and everything, and the harder it was to simply stay in the lighter moment of enjoying time with friends or family. Saying that everything was fine to a trusted confidante when it wasn't not only felt disingenuous but also fuelled my sense of emotional isolation. How are our loved ones going to better understand what we're dealing with and how we're feeling if we don't share those things?

Regardless of how great it is to capitalize on the opportunity to vent to someone dear, a social occasion just isn't the ideal forum. Sharing darker details can hijack the general mood of the gathering, which I definitely didn't want to instigate. A very dear friend once asked me why she didn't know about a couple of difficult decisions I had to make. I simply responded that it didn't make for a great dinner topic.

The last contributor to this feeling of disconnection was the hardest one for me to get my head around. I thought it would be easy to communicate to my loved ones how deeply challenged I was to cope with this healthcare journey. It was not. I frequently struggled to make them understand. I came away from many interactions with the feeling that a loved one wouldn't have responded the way they did to something I shared if I had been successful.

This realization was extremely difficult for me to accept because, until this journey, I didn't imagine there could be any moment when I wasn't successful in getting the people in my life to understand. My relationships with my family and friends are my greatest blessing, and I treasure what I understand to be deep connections with them.

I only understood the disconnect once I was able to step far enough back from it. When I did, I realized the hard truth.

Firstly, my loved ones didn't want to hear of us hurting, so they would ask me to think positively, pursue fulfillment in other arenas, or count my blessings. These are all great strategies, but hearing them at a time when I was sharing an update or concern signalled to me that my loved one didn't want to hear anything more. So, contrary to their best intentions of getting me to think of other, more positive things, I would be hurt by what seemed to me to be a casual dismissal of the topic.

My emotional vulnerability coloured what I heard, and I had very specific feelings about the three platitudes.

1. It was my positivity that inspired some of our healthcare team to think I could be delusional—weren't my loved ones paying attention?
2. They couldn't possibly understand what we were going through if they felt career fulfillment could be anywhere near my list of priorities.
3. Considering my blessings was one of my most effective coping strategies, but being asked to consider them always made me feel that the individual didn't want to hear the negative.

What I wasn't able to see at the time was that a more likely explanation for the offered platitude was that my loved one was uncomfortable discussing the topic. This thought should have occurred earlier, but I didn't recognize it. I couldn't recall any conversation about other adversities where my sharing was cut short. I wouldn't have felt so alone if my loved one had simply explained that they were having difficulty processing our challenges. I would have understood because I was in the same place.

My last insight is that it's unrealistic to expect someone to understand how deeply tested and consumed we are with our child's serious healthcare journey. In the acute phases involving chemo or hospitalizations, it's obvious to our loved ones that things are not right in our world. It's a lot less obvious that things are challenging when we aren't in an acute phase.

There's no way that someone who hasn't gone through something similar could possibly appreciate how close to the surface our fears and concerns are. The slightest scratch at the surface, through an appointment or a physical stumble, opens the floodgates to the fears.

Going for Hope

Once we were home from a hospitalization or rehab stay, it looked from the outside that things had returned to normal. As I described in the last chapter, our "normal" was irrevocably changed, and we had frequent reminders of the shift. Over time, you'd think it would become easier, but it doesn't because we keep gathering more and more evidence of how far-reaching the changes are. There isn't a single dimension of our lives that isn't impacted.

So the bottom line is this: As deeply as I wanted the same level of understanding I had received from my loved ones during other types of challenges, it was an unrealistic expectation for this particular challenge.

Feeling disconnected impacted me significantly enough that it was imperative that I figure out how to cope. This is where my strategies come in.

First, to create peace of mind, I needed to empathize with my loved ones. I appreciate if this seems backward to you because it certainly didn't occur to me for several years. It finally dawned on me that the only way someone would be able to understand me at the level I sought would be if they went through something similar. I couldn't wish that on anyone. Once I had this realization, the hurt of not feeling understood by some friends or family started to ease. I'm not saying there were no more moments of feeling alone in my understanding, but it no longer stung as much. I realized that it wasn't a conscious choice to not understand.

Embracing this strategy has only brought me peace. It hasn't stopped me from offering insights into our journey or my feelings. But when an opportunity to share arises, I'm not as deeply attached to their response.

Feeling understood remained important to me, though. As a result, I embraced a second strategy to deal with any sense of emotional isolation. I connected with individuals with a similar lived experience.

During the first year of this journey, we encountered many families across Cai's hospitalizations and rehabilitation. Understandably, the acute aspects of our care in these arenas limited both my interest in and my time for any meaningful connection. Consequently, our interactions were limited to smiles, nods, or brief hellos.

For the next couple of years, we would cross paths with other families as we attended follow-up appointments or therapy sessions. I simply didn't have the emotional bandwidth to look beyond our personal experience and pursue meaningful conversations with these families.

Cai's second protocol of chemotherapy began almost two years after diagnosis. As a result, we were in a hospital environment on a weekly basis and had frequent reminders of the services available to families like ours. We also had hours and hours of time available to start striking up conversations with the families waiting beside us.

After our first year on this chemo protocol, I was finally ready to consider applying for our family to attend a special and highly-valued Family Camp for families dealing with childhood cancer. It may sound odd, but completing the application process takes both attention and energy. Up until this point in time, I didn't feel like there was any additional energy to apply, let alone inspire me to leave my comfort zone.

It was during our first week of camp at Camp Trillium (now Campfire Circle[6]) that there was both the environment and the time for me to connect more meaningfully with other families.

In the earlier years, I'm pretty sure that this summer respite meant even more to me than it did to my kids. Yes, they did get to participate in a lot of fun activities, and they each had a special friend (counsellor) assigned to them who

---

[6] For more information, visit https://campfirecircle.org/

was entrusted with creating a great experience for them. But I had the amazing gift of relating to other parents who had suffered similar traumas. We parents were from all walks of life, and we could connect at a meaningful level after one conversation. They absolutely understood what it meant to be pushed so far outside of our comfort zone that we felt like fish out of water.

I cherished every single moment of our time at Camp and came away from each experience rejuvenated. I laughed harder in five days than I would have laughed in the several months leading up to it. We could speak to each other in shorthand. No explanations were required and empathy was overflowing. What a most wonderful gift. I'm so very thankful I took the plunge.

I think that feeling emotionally isolated goes hand-in-hand with a challenging adversity. As mentioned above, even people going through the same journey together can feel like the individual(s) on the journey with them don't "get" what they're feeling.

Empathizing with my loved ones reduced the intensity of my sense of disconnection. It also brought me peace of mind and made it possible to make the most of my moments with them. Making connections with individuals who had similar lived experiences was uplifting. My challenges were understood, and my feelings were validated.

These two strategies have been instrumental in me making the most of my moments with "my people." And yes, the more consistently positive interactions with them have fundamentally increased my sense of well-being.

Practically Speaking, When Disconnected

When feeling disconnected from your social supports:

1. Take a deep breath so you can remind yourself of the following: Don't take what may appear to be a lack of compassion personally—it is impossible for someone who hasn't gone through the same significant adversity to truly "get it!" This does *not* detract from the other ways your relationship with them is special.
2. Persevere by sharing what you're feeling or how you're challenged by your journey to the people in your circle, but don't be attached to a specific response.
3. Actively search out individuals facing similar challenges. Involved specialists are often more than happy to provide potential connections if you just ask. You can also speak with a therapist or research online to find support groups.
4. Remain open to sharing. The families I specifically reached out to to discuss "The New Normal" are the moms I met while our similarly aged daughters participated in a study regarding the social impacts of brain tumours. They are relationships I continue to value years after our first meeting. We still find ways to connect.

Long-Term Impacts of Stress

The Importance of Nurturing Your Emotional Well-Being

On journeys of great adversity, both hopefulness and resilience are critical. If we're hopeful, we'll take the most constructive and productive action. If we're resilient, we'll bounce back up after being knocked down. There is a difference between having a skill and having the bandwidth to exercise that skill. I'll do my best to share what I mean by my distinction.

A friend of mine refers to our two-decade healthcare journey as "living on the savannah." I can't take credit for the expression, but it certainly rings true. She described it this way because we have lived under what seems to be an ever-present level of alert. In this state, an enormous amount of emotional energy is consumed, which I have learned has negatively impacted my bandwidth for hopefulness and resilience over time.

Accepting our new normal and dealing with my feelings of isolation used up a significant amount of my emotional energy. And that was true before other interventions were required. Unfortunately, the likelihood of a child needing additional interventions due to long-term health issues resulting from their treatments is high.

This is one of the ways that Cailyn's journey is not exceptional. Her follow-ups and interventions in many disciplines extend well into the second decade of her journey. A brief synopsis, not listed chronologically, includes:

1. Her tumour has progressed four times in the years since her brain surgeries and rehabilitation at Holland Bloorview. The first two progressions resulted in over six years of weekly chemotherapy. The third progression required consultations to determine what course of action we were going to take. I decided to defer starting treatment until after the holidays that year and wanted one more MRI to confirm that treatment was necessary. Thankfully, we were blessed with a stable MRI early the next February. We celebrated the stable result, but it did nothing to quell the anxiety I experienced for each of her next scans. And it was just two years later that the dimensions of her tumour grew significantly again. This time, she was closer to eighteen years old, and the hope was that her tumour would become quiescent (dormant) as her hormones stabilized. I held my breath as we walked the tightrope between the available interventions with their associated risks and the emotionally and physically devastating development of more symptoms and deficits if the tumour continued to grow. Again, we chose the do-nothing option and anxiously awaited our quarterly MRIs, hoping we hadn't made the wrong decision.
2. Cailyn has had two eye surgeries to address the misalignment in her eyes due to muscle weakness resulting from neurological deficits. The first surgery wasn't successful, so a second surgery was required three years

later. Unexpectedly, her post-surgical double vision never resolved, so she's had to learn how to accommodate, which she has done with great grace. She has had innumerable follow-ups with her ophthalmologist to stay on top of both the positioning of her eyes and the quality of her vision.
3. As a result of her left-sided hemiplegia, she has just had her fifth surgery on her left foot and ankle. Each surgery has required her to be non-weight-bearing for significant periods of time post-surgery and necessitated ongoing physiotherapy. Witnessing your child's devastation over the difficult news that yet another surgery is required for pain reduction is heartbreaking. Cai's devastation resulted in me wondering just how much someone can endure, especially when there seems to be no foreseeable fix.

Through all the challenges faced in the first few years of her medical journey, I was able to get myself to my "happy spot," the hopeful frame of mind that Cailyn's long-term health concerns would be a thing of the past. When her tumour first progressed, a year and a half after her surgery in New York, I told anyone who would listen that the chemo regimen she was put on was going to destroy the tumour. That was the perspective that made it possible to stay in a hopeful zone.

This *first* progression in her tumour led to two years of weekly chemotherapy. Regardless of my sustained belief that the chemotherapy would work to erase it, the tumour hadn't changed discernibly. It was time to give Cai's body a break, though, so we stopped her weekly treatments. It was absolutely the right thing to do, but it felt like we were giving up our safety net. I dreaded the next MRI. Would they find evidence that we should have continued treatment?

Scan anxiety is something that every single family I've met on this type of journey experiences. Once you've been on the receiving end of very difficult and unexpected news, you accept that there's no guarantee that your child is protected from receiving more negative news. Having to start chemotherapy a year and a half after her surgery in New York provided proof of this point. On top of our own experience, the risk of further growth is actually part of the dialogue we have with our medical professionals. And, unfortunately, we sit beside and meet many families in hospital waiting rooms that share their horror stories of their child's tumour progression or relapse.

So when we stopped Cailyn's weekly chemotherapy about four years after the original diagnosis, I was painfully aware that her tumour's stability at that moment did not guarantee its stability going forward. I was keenly aware that it could just be a matter of time.

In the six months (and two MRIs) following this break from chemotherapy, I had four sinus infections. I would conservatively estimate that each week, I was either in the middle of an illness or I felt like I was getting sick.

It was near the end of my fourth sinus infection that the movement of my eyes felt different. I initially excused it as a by-product of my latest sinus infection, but it was different enough that I booked an appointment with our optometrist. She confirmed that my vision was stable, and, not finding a reason for concern, I thought that the weird feeling would pass as I healed from the latest illness.

Unfortunately, I was wrong. The weird movement of my eyes progressed to me experiencing double vision. This was a symptom that was much harder to ignore, so the search to determine the root cause continued. Almost a year later and six days before Christmas, after several months of appointments and tests, I received the news that I, too, had a brain tumour. It was a different type and location than Cailyn's, but those facts didn't seem too pertinent at the time.

There's no way to be 100 percent sure, but I believe that the biggest contributor to the development of my brain tumour was chronic stress. As shared, our bodies aren't designed to deal with a constant, elevated level of stress. I share this simply to support the importance of actively putting some priority on seeking out and using strategies to release stress. I did not excel along this dimension. I feel that my diagnosis was a sign that my physical resilience was low.

Up until this moment of the healthcare journey, the majority of my energy was focused on my children's needs. There was no question in my mind that their needs should take priority over any self-care activity.

I don't believe embracing strategies to actively support health and well-being will result in perfect health, but I now believe it can be a key contributor to the best outcomes possible. Finding strategies for actively coping with a chronic stressor should have appeared somewhere on my list of priorities.

Getting a diagnosis of a brain tumour definitely got my attention, and I amplified my efforts to eat cleanly. We already ate very carefully, but I bought and implemented strategies from a book called *Anti-Cancer: A New Way of Life* by Dr. David Servan Schreiber. I totally embraced the insights shared on cancer-fighting strategies and foods, and I felt there was more than one of us in the house who would benefit from the wisdom in the book.

I'm confident now, and I was confident then that improving our diet was a significant contributor to a better level of health. It required enough of my time and attention to plan and prepare our meals that this was the only strategy I consciously implemented. I was hopeful that it was all that was needed to be done.

For approximately the next year and a half, my focus was on all our commitments and obligations, including dozens of follow-up appointments and MRIs for both Cailyn and me. As long as my symptoms didn't worsen, we carried on.

Several weeks before one of my follow-up MRIs, I noticed I was experiencing double vision again. My vision had been "back to normal" up until this time. A fascinating fact about brain tumours is that if the tumour is stable, symptoms can fade as the brain learns to adapt to the pressure put on the brain cells and nerves surrounding a tumour. When the sense of double vision became more evident again, I wondered if it was because there had been a noticeable change in the dimensions of the tumour.

I said nothing to my family about the recurrence of my double vision. I felt I could just wait to learn what the MRI had to reveal. I wasn't surprised to hear that the tumour had grown. What I was surprised about was that it had doubled in size. This is when the conversation about radiation began.

It was emotionally stressful to even consider this option. Radiation was an intervention that had been tabled for Cailyn and quickly rejected because of potential long-term consequences. As a result, I was very sensitive to the potential risks I might face. Considering the location of my tumour, gamma-knife radiation was preferable to surgery. So, later that summer, I underwent radiation.

I found the treatment to be very traumatic. I was "fitted" with a headframe, whose installation caused a level of pain that was temporarily mind-numbing. As the day wore on, I became nauseous from the sustained discomfort, likely exacerbated by the preparatory scans and frequent manipulation of the frame to ensure it was still secure. I had to wear the headframe for approximately eight hours before my turn came, and then I was in the active phase of receiving radiation for over two and a half hours.

Going for Hope

I remember telling myself that Cailyn had had to deal with so much more while I was still lying in the machine, rubbing my rock with the word "hope" imprinted on it. The enormity of this thought brought tears to my eyes, and by the time the treatment was completed, the tears were rolling down my face. When the head frame was removed, I was literally and figuratively *done*.

It took several weeks for this feeling of being done, both emotionally and physically, to ease. When I felt more like myself, we were well into a new school year, with its associated activities and appointments.

Flash forward a few months, and we learned about Cailyn's *second* tumour progression through one of her follow-up MRIs. More intervention was required. I think this is the moment that my steadfast hopefulness started to crumble. The biggest contributor to this crumbling was sheer exhaustion. In this state, finding my way to my happy place, where I was confident everything was going to work out, eluded me.

Every strategy used prior to this moment helped me navigate traumatic moments along our journey. They were constructive actions powered by my hopefulness that the action could facilitate an improved situation. I believe that my capacity to take action was fuelled by the emotional energy needed to manufacture hope and resilience. After this progression in Cai's tumour, my emotional energy flickered.

A thought I couldn't ignore after the progression was that the two-year weekly chemotherapy regimen had been ineffective at stopping Cailyn's tumour from growing. As a result, the hope I had when starting the previous regimen—that the chemo would either erase the tumour, decrease its size, or stop it from growing—was eroded, if not entirely evaporated.

Chemotherapy was still the lesser of the evils in terms of the risk of long-term effects, but there was no ignoring that there would be a cost to Cailyn's long-term health and well-being arising from more chemo. And this cost might not be revealed for years. Not a comforting thought. Another difficult thing to swallow was that there wasn't a proven, long-term algorithm for dealing with brain tumours like Cailyn's.

Regardless of our fears or misgivings, we began weekly chemo again, not knowing how long she'd have to be on it. As it turned out, she remained on it for over four years.

The length of the chemo regimen that Cai was on was seventy weeks. Her first round with this drug was two years, and her second round was four. Why not seventy weeks, you ask? Well, the history of developments experienced along Cai's journey was unique, and when our experiences were considered in light of the horrible location of her tumour and her developmental age, there wasn't a clear course of action. A serious contributor to staying on the regimen was the hope that if we got her far enough beyond the onset of puberty, it could help decrease the risk of further growth after coming off of it. What was really tough for me to accept was that the chemo was never viewed as a cure; it was simply a means to hold the growth of the tumour steady, hopefully long enough to enable it to get to a dormant stage.

I remember a friend of mine observing, during this four-year interval, that my adrenal glands must be completely shot. Our bodies just aren't designed to deal with a long, enduring level of life-threatening or quality-of-life-threatening stress. I honestly wasn't sure what to make of the comment, but I knew I felt physically, mentally, and emotionally drained.

It took me a few years to learn that my emotional energy was the gatekeeper of my physical and mental energy. I also learned that, for me, resilience, hopefulness, and positive action are inextricably linked. Taking positive action requires the hopefulness that the action can make a difference; resilience is required to get back up after being knocked down, and both of these qualities require emotional energy. Without it, much less of substance is accomplished. I had this a-ha insight when I finally realized that for the first few days after a healthcare appointment for Cailyn, I felt like I didn't have it in me to care for anything of substance beyond my girls' needs: food, transportation to school and activities, homework support, etc.

Any longer-term pursuits were, at best, on the back burner, if not altogether invisible to me. It was like I had zero bandwidth to consider anything that wasn't urgent to my girls' everyday needs. And it was fascinating how quickly an idea for a book or a blog entry would vanish. I don't know how many times I conceptualized what I thought would be a great blog entry driving home from an errand, only to lose the train of thought by the time I got home.

I have learned to respect the huge role that emotional energy plays by living through the consequences of it running low. Take too many cups of coffee out of the pot without actively finding ways to fill it up again, and the pot runs dry. The source of energy to continue sparking hopefulness and resilience is compromised.

I wonder if I might have avoided my own diagnosis of a brain tumour if I had known what the cost of chronic emotional trauma could be. In the moment, our real challenges and the multitudinous what-ifs completely obscured any thought of self-care.

Thankfully, I've learned a great deal about the importance of consciously embracing things like exercise, meditation, and yoga to build my health and well-being. Building the strength of my connections with my support circle has also had a fundamental impact on my overall health.

As I rebuild my energy stores, both my resilience and hopefulness are more present allies and the actions necessary to create lemonade are clearer. My goal is to never take my well-being for granted again!

Practically Speaking, When Dealing with Long-Term Impacts of Stress

Here are a few strategies to have on your radar for your own health and well-being:

1. When you're experiencing significant duress, you have to make a commitment to put on your own oxygen mask. Proactively focusing on your health and well-being reduces the potential that matters will be taken out of your own hands.
2. Deep breathing (breathe in for four seconds, hold for four, and release for seven or eight)—this can be done at almost any time and in almost any location. It's amazing how many times the phrase that comes to mind when I'm actively doing deep breathing is, "I can do this!"
3. Choose at least one of the following actions per day:
   a. Connect with someone who brings you joy, makes you laugh, gives you a genuine hug, or inspires you to do positive things for yourself. This doesn't have to be an in-person get-together.
   b. Some cardio—walking, biking, running, swimming, etc. On really busy days, choose the activity that takes the least amount of prep time, or that combines more than one "to-do" item. Walking the dog is one of my go-to's. I have convinced myself that physical exertion is one of the best ways to release built-up stress.

c. An activity that focuses on your strength and balance—yoga, weight-lifting, or pilates. There are many days when getting down on the floor to do yoga or pilates doesn't seem possible for me. I have convinced myself that doing a series of stairs can be a great option.
d. Meditation—I find meditation hard to do for more than a couple of minutes. My personalized approach is to pair deep breathing with either listing what I'm grateful for as I breathe out or reciting my vision board elements. I know it isn't actually meditation, but it does ensure that I'm focused on only positive things for a period of time.
e. Avoid negative energy. It's so hard to remain in a hopeful state of mind when drowning in a sea of negativity. I think it's a bit unrealistic to suggest we can avoid all sources of negative energy. However, it is in our power to actively seek out positive additions to our day. If you look at my social media feeds, you will find a predominant proportion of good news stories, comedy routines, and reels featuring dogs and babies, talent show performances, baking demonstrations, volleyball clips, and health-promoting wisdom. The thing I try hardest to limit is exposure to a negativity over which I have no control to change. Healthcare challenges already fill up that particular box.

Afterword:
My Most Important Takeaways

AKA... The Takeaways I'm Most Hopeful You'll Remember

I'd like to kick off this final chapter with an interaction I had with my child's diagnosing doctor several years into our journey. He saw Cai skipping down the hall and commented on how well she was doing. He shared that he didn't believe in miracles—he didn't use the "M"-word—but that Cai's recovery was miraculous. I believe the majority of Cai's medical team views her recovery as exceptional. I'm not saying there haven't been longer-term challenges, but the fact that she's here and as able as she is is extraordinary.

As Paul Harvey would say, "Now you know the rest of the story....".

I coined a phrase over a decade ago: "Life is about growth: adversity inspires it and hope fuels it." It's a mantra I have used over and over. I'd like to share what it means to me.

I've wondered about the meaning of life, and our challenges have put a spotlight on this question. I've come away from my reflection believing that a critical component of living is growth. Hence, the first part of the saying "Life is about growth."

I don't think anyone gets to opt out of adversities in their life. I think they're one of life's "givens." We may not know what someone else is dealing with, but that doesn't mean there isn't something pushing them beyond their comfort zone.

I don't have the ability to control what comes into our lives, but I do have the ability to control how I respond to it. At a high level, my response can fit into one of two buckets. I can see the basket of lemons only as a burden to carry, or I can make a conscious decision to try to create the sweetest lemonade possible. For me, adversity can act as the inspiration I need to rise to a challenge with the aim of creating the best possible outcome, or it can shut me down. Striving towards an improved outcome in an adverse situation requires me to grow to meet the challenge. I don't know if there's a stronger motivator for growth than adversity.

The last critical component of my mantra brings in the essential quality of hope. If I had to choose the quality most responsible for the exceptional results realized on our journey, it would be hope. It is the basis upon which all of my constructive and productive actions were taken. I couldn't begin to estimate the number of positive actions I took simply because I was hopeful they would improve the situation. "Hope fuels it!"

Going for Hope

In my mind, the relationship between growth, adversity, and hope is incontrovertible.

There is absolutely no condition under which I would have welcomed the challenges my daughter has had to face along this crazy healthcare journey. Regardless, it has also brought blessings. I'll admit that it wasn't easy to acknowledge our blessings when I was hanging on by my fingertips. But whenever I did acknowledge them, it felt like I was receiving a hand-up.

Some of the blessings are in the form of increased strengths, improved self-awareness, and clarity regarding what's important. Other blessings are in the form of exceptional support. Some of this is provided by individuals, and some by organizations. The shared intent is to lift us up and remind us that we're not alone. No words can express how emotionally and positively impactful these gestures were. Prior to diagnosis, there was no way we could have anticipated the incredible level of support that was going to come our way as a result of the adversity.

These blessings were injections of positive energy, and as such, they shored up my capacity to cope. The strategies I've shared in this book were also instrumental in my capacity to cope. I encourage anyone dealing with a challenging situation to pay attention to the actions that help them most. When an action is the catalyst to move forward with hope, it's a critical coping strategy. These strategies are essential allies through *any* adversity. You don't need to be facing a life-threatening brain tumour.

My strategies came to me at times of desperation. They aren't exceptional in the sense that there's no rocket science behind them, but they are exceptional for the outcomes they enabled. An improved state of mind was not the least of these outcomes.

Unfortunately, as I shared in the previous chapter, the longer the journey goes on, the emptier the well of emotional energy becomes. The preceding chapter provides you with some insight into how impactful an unrelenting journey can be.

How do the strategies affect hopefulness and resilience? Immeasurably! This answer is valid in either the acute or chronic phases of our journey.

In the acute phase, the most important reason for me to use a particular strategy was to protect my hopefulness. If I was hopeful, I was more likely to take the most constructive action. If I wasn't hopeful, I was more likely to simply accept the situation we were dealt.

In the chronic phase, the most important reason for me to consciously use a strategy was to nurture resilience. It's clear to me that any wavering hopefulness on my part had everything to do with my declining resilience.

One of my biggest shortcomings was my inability to initially see and acknowledge how critical coping strategies were during the chronic phase. In the acute phase, when the pressure seemed most intense, it was crystal clear to me that I had to grasp something—anything—to hold on to. These strategies made it possible to endure the situation. When the situations were less intense, I didn't respect how fundamentally these strategies would shore up my resilience over the long term and protect my capacity to be hopeful.

What I know now is that the use of conscientious strategies facilitated the most positive outcomes during our acute phase. I wish I had used them as conscientiously during the more chronic phase. The "rest of the story" affirms that strategies and the hopefulness to use them can contribute to phenomenal outcomes.

Moving along a "journey of a lifetime" doesn't just challenge you; it changes you. These changes run the gamut, from

Going for Hope

very positive to very negative, from mental to physical to emotional to spiritual. I believe that it's impossible to remain unmarked by the experiences along the way. We can do things to mitigate how scarring they are, but tipping the scales away from baggage and towards blessings requires conscientious effort, effective strategies, and an expenditure of emotional energy.

I hope my experience can help you get into the zone of "can do" and "will do." I know first-hand how difficult this can be to achieve.

Ann Hovey

The Strategies that Make It Possible to Persevere

- Ask for H-E-L-P! Needing help is not a sign of weakness. When life challenges you, asking for help demonstrates your commitment to doing what you can to facilitate a positive outcome.
- Go for hope! There are no guarantees in life, so you might as well remain hopeful that your positive and constructive action will move you towards your desired outcome. Belief is a powerful motivator!
- Focus on what you can control. We can't control what happens to us, but we can control how we respond to it. There is always something you can do to positively impact a difficult situation. Protect your power to remain hopeful.
- Stay in the moment. Your power to act, your ability to experience joy, and your capacity to feel peace are available only in this particular moment… not in the past and not in the future. Don't let what-ifs derail your focus from what you can do to make the most of a moment.
- Deal with conflicts. Issues don't resolve themselves. Determine what action is required to address the conflict successfully and commit to following through. You're worth the effort!
- Embrace the mindset of possibility. Choose empowerment over victimhood. Focus on a goal that is important to you and determine what things you can do to drive towards it. Don't be afraid to be relentless because you have nothing to lose!
- Find and count your blessings. Pair your blessings with deep breathing exercises for the most positive impact on your mindset and well-being.

- Focus on the right step to take in the moment. Persevering happens one moment at a time. The next best step will reveal itself.
- Use the five by five rule: if it isn't going to be an issue in five years, it's not worth spending more than five minutes worrying about it now.
- Black box it! Strengths are difficult to see in the face of fear, worry, insecurity. Take the distracting insecurities and worries and lock them away so you can see what strengths you can bring to the present moment.
- Make connecting socially a priority. Be realistic about the support you can expect from your loved ones. Be thankful for the care and friendship they do provide. Search out individuals with a similar lived experience.
- Prioritize your well-being. Fight the long-term impacts of stress by staying active and surrounding yourself with positive energy.
- Above all, embrace the growth that will be required to navigate your adversity successfully and with grace. Respect the pivotal role that hope plays in fuelling that growth.
- Remember, the best actions are powered by hopeful intention.

Acknowledgments

Above all, I want to recognize Cailyn for her capacity to persevere and rise in the face of innumerable difficulties. Cai—you are inspirational to anyone blessed to know you!

I want to thank Lauryn for the love, caring, and joy she injected into our moments and the patience she demonstrated beyond her years. Lo—your empathy is a gift to anyone in your circle.

To my parents, thank you for your unwavering presence and support across too many challenges to count. You were my rocks when I felt surrounded by quicksand.

I want to thank Rob Todd for her belief in my work and her encouragement to keep writing. Your support was given across many dimensions and has been instrumental in the realization of this book!

I will forever be grateful to the medical specialists, therapists, and support staff who did everything they could to contribute their skills, experience, wisdom, and care to my child's health and well-being. We are so very fortunate you were on our team.

I also want to thank the publishing team at Igniting Souls for managing every component of publishing—an arena I know absolutely nothing about.

There have been several family members and friends who have read a little or a lot of this book and encouraged me to keep going. I'm so very thankful for your support of me and your belief in my book. Every encouragement inspired me.

Finally, to the families beside whom we've walked our treacherous path, thank you for your input to two of my Chronic Phase chapters. It has been an honour to walk with you.

About the Author

Ann Hovey is an author, speaker, facilitator, coach, and mother. Ann's educational background in Engineering and Statistics affirmed her appreciation for data and process, while her professional experiences have reinforced the power of soft skills when striving for optimal results.

Professionally, she has had the privilege of facilitating successful problem-solving and relationship-building sessions, significant improvements in process quality, and company-wide reorganizational activities. She has also held a leadership role in implementing an internal organizational coaching process for employees.

In all areas of life, Ann firmly believes in the power of teams to achieve exceptional outcomes when individual perspectives are respected and everyone pulls in the same direction. Her perspectives were shaped in part by her years playing and helping coach volleyball at the university level. She maintains that every individual brings something unique to the world, and her mission is to help individuals gain confidence in their ability to create their most fulfilling life.

Personally and professionally, Ann has come to deeply understand the lengths to which adversity can push people. She has been a relentless advocate for her daughter during her healthcare journey. This journey inspired her to create and deliver presentations to medical personnel on how to successfully partner with caregivers for optimal results. She has also developed workshops and presentations on her strategies for facing adversity.

Ann has two daughters, Cailyn and Lauryn.

GOING FOR HOPE

Visit AnnHovey.com for additional content, bonus material, opportunities, and more.

AnnHovey.com

THIS BOOK IS PROTECTED INTELLECTUAL PROPERTY

The author of this book values Intellectual Property. The book you just read is protected by Instant IP™, a proprietary process, which integrates blockchain technology giving Intellectual Property "Global Protection." By creating a "Time-Stamped" smart contract that can never be tampered with or changed, we establish "First Use" that tracks back to the author.

Instant IP™ functions much like a Pre-Patent™ since it provides an immutable "First Use" of the Intellectual Property. This is achieved through our proprietary process of leveraging blockchain technology and smart contracts. As a result, proving "First Use" is simple through a global and verifiable smart contract. By protecting intellectual property with blockchain technology and smart contracts, we establish a "First to File" event.

Protected by Instant IP™

LEARN MORE AT INSTANTIP.TODAY

www.ingramcontent.com/pod-product-compliance
Lightning Source LLC
Chambersburg PA
CBHW052145070526
44585CB00017B/1983